AWS Certificate Manager User Guide

A catalogue record for this book is available from the Hong Kong Public Libraries.

Published in Hong Kong by Samurai Media Limited.

Email: info@samuraimedia.org

ISBN 9789888407941

Contents

What Is AWS Certificate Manager?

Welcome to the AWS Certificate Manager (ACM) service. ACM handles the complexity of creating and managing public SSL/TLS certificates for your AWS based websites and applications. You can use public certificates provided by ACM (ACM certificates) or certificates that you import into ACM. ACM certificates can secure multiple domain names and multiple names within a domain. You can also use ACM to create wildcard SSL certificates that can protect an unlimited number of subdomains.

ACM is tightly linked with AWS Certificate Manager Private Certificate Authority. You can use ACM PCA to create a private certificate authority (CA) and then use ACM to issue private certificates. These are SSL/TLS X.509 certificates that identify users, computers, applications, services, servers, and other devices internally. Private certificates cannot be publicly trusted. For more information about ACM PCA, see the AWS Certificate Manager Private Certificate Authority User Guide. Private certificates issued by using ACM are much like public ACM certificates. They have similar benefits and restrictions. The benefits include managing the private keys associated with the certificate, renewing certificates, and enabling you to use the console to deploy your private certificate with integrated services. For more information about the restrictions associated with using ACM, see Request a Private Certificate. You can also use ACM to export a private certificate and encrypted private key to use anywhere. For more information, see Export a Private Certificate. For information about the benefits of using ACM PCA as a standalone service to issue private certificates, see the introduction in the ACM PCA User Guide.

Note
You cannot install public ACM certificates directly on your website or application. You must install your certificate by using one of the services integrated with ACM and ACM PCA. For more information about these services, see Services Integrated with AWS Certificate Manager.

Topics

- Concepts
- ACM Certificate Characteristics
- Supported Regions
- Integrated Services
- Site Seals and Trust Logos
- Limits
- Best Practices
- Pricing

Concepts

This section introduces basic terms and concepts related to AWS Certificate Manager (ACM).

Topics

- ACM Certificate
- Apex Domain
- Asymmetric Key Cryptography
- Certificate Authority
- Certificate Transparency Logging
- Domain Name System
- Domain Names
- Encryption and Decryption
- Fully Qualified Domain Name (FQDN)
- Public Key Infrastructure
- Root Certificate
- Secure Sockets Layer (SSL)
- Secure HTTPS
- SSL Server Certificates
- Symmetric Key Cryptography
- Transport Layer Security (TLS)
- Trust

ACM Certificate

ACM generates X.509 version 3 certificates. Each is valid for 13 months and contains the following extensions.

- **Basic Constraints**- specifies whether the subject of the certificate is a certification authority (CA)
- **Authority Key Identifier**- enables identification of the public key corresponding to the private key used to sign the certificate.
- **Subject Key Identifier**- enables identification of certificates that contain a particular public key.
- **Key Usage**- defines the purpose of the public key embedded in the certificate.
- **Extended Key Usage**- specifies one or more purposes for which the public key may be used in addition to the purposes specified by the **Key Usage** extension.
- **CRL Distribution Points**- specifies where CRL information can be obtained.

```
1  Certificate:
2      Data:
3          Version: 3 (0x2)
4          Serial Number:
5              f2:16:ad:85:d8:42:d1:8a:3f:33:fa:cc:c8:50:a8:9e
6      Signature Algorithm: sha256WithRSAEncryption
7          Issuer: O=Example CA
8          Validity
9              Not Before: Jan 30 18:46:53 2018 GMT
10             Not After : Jan 31 19:46:53 2018 GMT
11         Subject: C=US, ST=VA, L=Herndon, O=Amazon, OU=AWS, CN=example.com
12         Subject Public Key Info:
13             Public Key Algorithm: rsaEncryption
14                 Public-Key: (2048 bit)
15                 Modulus:
16                     00:ba:a6:8a:aa:91:0b:63:e8:08:de:ca:e7:59:a4:
17                     69:4c:e9:ea:26:04:d5:31:54:f5:ec:cb:4e:af:27:
18                     e3:94:0f:a6:85:41:6b:8e:a3:c1:c8:c0:3f:1c:ac:
```

```
19          a2:ca:0a:b2:dd:7f:c0:57:53:0b:9f:b4:70:78:d5:
20          43:20:ef:2c:07:5a:e4:1f:d1:25:24:4a:81:ab:d5:
21          08:26:73:f8:a6:d7:22:c2:4f:4f:86:72:0e:11:95:
22          03:96:6d:d5:3f:ff:18:a6:0b:36:c5:4f:78:bc:51:
23          b5:b6:36:86:7c:36:65:6f:2e:82:73:1f:c7:95:85:
24          a4:77:96:3f:c0:96:e2:02:94:64:f0:3a:df:e0:76:
25          05:c4:56:a2:44:72:6f:8a:8a:a1:f3:ee:34:47:14:
26          bc:32:f7:50:6a:e9:42:f5:f4:1c:9a:7a:74:1d:e5:
27          68:09:75:19:4b:ac:c6:33:90:97:8c:0d:d1:eb:8a:
28          02:f3:3e:01:83:8d:16:f6:40:39:21:be:1a:72:d8:
29          5a:15:68:75:42:3e:f0:0d:54:16:ed:9a:8f:94:ec:
30          59:25:e0:37:8e:af:6a:6d:99:0a:8d:7d:78:0f:ea:
31          40:6d:3a:55:36:8e:60:5b:d6:0d:b4:06:a3:ac:ab:
32          e2:bf:c9:b7:fe:22:9e:2a:f6:f3:42:bb:94:3e:b7:
33          08:73
34      Exponent: 65537 (0x10001)
35  X509v3 extensions:
36      X509v3 Basic Constraints:
37          CA:FALSE
38      X509v3 Authority Key Identifier:
39          keyid:84:8C:AC:03:A2:38:D9:B6:81:7C:DF:F1:95:C3:28:31:D5:F7:88:42
40      X509v3 Subject Key Identifier:
41          97:06:15:F1:EA:EC:07:83:4C:19:A9:2F:AF:BA:BB:FC:B2:3B:55:D8
42      X509v3 Key Usage: critical
43          Digital Signature, Key Encipherment
44      X509v3 Extended Key Usage:
45          TLS Web Server Authentication, TLS Web Client Authentication
46      X509v3 CRL Distribution Points:
47          Full Name:
48            URI:http://example.com/crl
49
50  Signature Algorithm: sha256WithRSAEncryption
51      69:03:15:0c:fb:a9:39:a3:30:63:b2:d4:fb:cc:8f:48:a3:46:
52      69:60:a7:33:4a:f4:74:88:c6:b6:b6:b8:ab:32:c2:a0:98:c6:
53      8d:f0:8f:b5:df:78:a1:5b:02:18:72:65:bb:53:af:2f:3a:43:
54      76:3c:9d:d4:35:a2:e2:1f:29:11:67:80:29:b9:fe:c9:42:52:
55      cb:6d:cd:d0:e2:2f:16:26:19:cd:f7:26:c5:dc:81:40:3b:e3:
56      d1:b0:7e:ba:80:99:9a:5f:dd:92:b0:bb:0c:32:dd:68:69:08:
57      e9:3c:41:2f:15:a7:53:78:4d:33:45:17:3e:f2:f1:45:6b:e7:
58      17:d4:80:41:15:75:ed:c3:d4:b5:e3:48:8d:b5:0d:86:d4:7d:
59      94:27:62:84:d8:98:6f:90:1e:9c:e0:0b:fa:94:cc:9c:ee:3a:
60      8a:6e:6a:9d:ad:b8:76:7b:9a:5f:d1:a5:4f:d0:b7:07:f8:1c:
61      03:e5:3a:90:8c:bc:76:c9:96:f0:4a:31:65:60:d8:10:fc:36:
62      44:8a:c1:fb:9c:33:75:fe:a6:08:d3:89:81:b0:6f:c3:04:0b:
63      a3:04:a1:d1:1c:46:57:41:08:40:b1:38:f9:57:62:97:10:42:
64      8e:f3:a7:a8:77:26:71:74:c2:0a:5b:9e:cc:d5:2c:c5:27:c3:
65      12:b9:35:d5
```

Apex Domain

See Domain Names.

Asymmetric Key Cryptography

Unlike Symmetric Key Cryptography, asymmetric cryptography uses different but mathematically related keys to encrypt and decrypt content. One of the keys is public and is typically made available in an X.509 v3 certificate. The other key is private and is stored securely. The X.509 certificate binds the identity of a user, computer, or other resource (the certificate subject) to the public key.

ACM Certificates are X.509 SSL/TLS certificates that bind the identity of your website and the details of your organization to the public key that is contained in the certificate. ACM stores the associated private key in a hardware security module (HSM).

Certificate Authority

A certificate authority (CA) is an entity that issues digital certificates. Commercially, the most common type of digital certificate is based on the ISO X.509 standard. The CA issues signed digital certificates that affirm the identity of the certificate subject and bind that identity to the public key contained in the certificate. A CA also typically manages certificate revocation.

Certificate Transparency Logging

To guard against SSL/TLS certificates that are issued by mistake or by a compromised CA, some browsers require that public certificates issued for your domain be recorded in a certificate transparency log. The domain name is recorded. The private key is not. Certificates that are not logged typically generate an error in the browser.

You can monitor the logs to make sure that only certificates you have authorized have been issued for your domain. You can use a service such as Certificate Search to check the logs.

Before the Amazon CA issues a publicly trusted SSL/TLS certificate for your domain, it submits the certificate to at least two certificate transparency log servers. These servers add the certificate to their public databases and return a signed certificate timestamp (SCT) to the Amazon CA. The CA then embeds the SCT in the certificate, signs the certificate, and issues it to you. The timestamps are included with other X.509 extensions.

```
1   X509v3 extensions:
2
3     CT Precertificate SCTs:
4       Signed Certificate Timestamp:
5         Version   : v1(0)
6         Log ID    : BB:D9:DF:...8E:1E:D1:85
7         Timestamp : Apr 24 23:43:15.598 2018 GMT
8         Extensions: none
9         Signature : ecdsa-with-SHA256
10                    30:45:02:...18:CB:79:2F
11      Signed Certificate Timestamp:
12        Version   : v1(0)
13        Log ID    : 87:75:BF:...A0:83:0F
14        Timestamp : Apr 24 23:43:15.565 2018 GMT
15        Extensions: none
16        Signature : ecdsa-with-SHA256
17                    30:45:02:...29:8F:6C
```

Certificate transparency logging is automatic when you request or renew a certificate unless you choose to opt out. For more information about opt out, see Opting Out of Certificate Transparency Logging.

Domain Name System

The Domain Name System (DNS) is a hierarchical distributed naming system for computers and other resources connected to the internet or a private network. DNS is primarily used to translate textual domain names, such as `aws.amazon.com`, into numerical IP (Internet Protocol) addresses of the form `111.222.333.444`. The DNS database for your domain, however, contains a number of records that can be used for other purposes. For example, with ACM you can use a CNAME record to validate that you own or control a domain when you request a certificate. For more information, see Use DNS to Validate Domain Ownership.

Domain Names

A domain name is a text string such as `www.example.com` that can be translated by the Domain Name System (DNS) into an IP address. Computer networks, including the internet, use IP addresses rather than text names. A domain name consists of distinct labels separated by periods:

TLD
The rightmost label is called the top-level domain (TLD). Common examples include `.com`, `.net`, and `.edu`. Also, the TLD for entities registered in some countries is an abbreviation of the country name and is called a country code. Examples include `.uk` for the United Kingdom, `.ru` for Russia, and `.fr` for France. When country codes are used, a second-level hierarchy for the TLD is often introduced to identify the type of the registered entity. For example, the `.co.uk` TLD identifies commercial enterprises in the United Kingdom.

Apex domain
The apex domain name includes and expands on the top-level domain. For domain names that include a country code, the apex domain includes the code and the labels, if any, that identify the type of the registered entity. The apex domain does not include subdomains (see the following paragraph). In `www.example.com`, the name of the apex domain is `example.com`. In `www.example.co.uk`, the name of the apex domain is `example.co.uk`. Other names that are often used instead of apex include base, bare, root, root apex, or zone apex.

Subdomain
Subdomain names precede the apex domain name and are separated from it and from each other by a period. The most common subdomain name is `www`, but any name is possible. Also, subdomain names can have multiple levels. For example, in `jake.dog.animals.example.com`, the subdomains are `jake`, `dog`, and `animals` in that order.

FQDN
A fully qualified domain name (FQDN) is the complete DNS name for a computer, website, or other resource connected to a network or to the internet. For example `aws.amazon.com` is the FQDN for Amazon Web Services. An FQDN includes all domains up to the top–level domain. For example, `[subdomain1].[subdomain2]...[subdomainn].[apex domain].[toplevel domain]` represents the general format of an FQDN.

PQDN
A domain name that is not fully qualified is called a partially qualified domain name (PQDN) and is ambiguous. A name such as `[subdomain1.subdomain2.]` is a PQDN because the root domain cannot be determined.

Registration
The right to use a domain name is delegated by domain name registrars. Registrars are typically accredited by the Internet Corporation for Assigned Names and Numbers (ICANN). In addition, other organizations called registries maintain the TLD databases. When you request a domain name, the registrar sends your information to the appropriate TLD registry. The registry assigns a domain name, updates the TLD database, and publishes your information to WHOIS. Typically, domain names must be purchased.

Encryption and Decryption

Encryption is the process of providing data confidentiality. Decryption reverses the process and recovers the original data. Unencrypted data is typically called plaintext whether it is text or not. Encrypted data is typically called ciphertext. HTTPS encryption of messages between clients and servers uses algorithms and keys. Algorithms define the step-by-step procedure by which plaintext data is converted into ciphertext (encryption) and ciphertext is converted back into the original plaintext (decryption). Keys are used by algorithms during the encryption or decryption process. Keys can be either private or public.

Fully Qualified Domain Name (FQDN)

See Domain Names.

Public Key Infrastructure

A public key infrastructure (PKI) consists of hardware, software, people, policies, documents, and procedures that are needed to create, issue, manage, distribute, use, store, and revoke digital certificates. PKI facilitates the secure transfer of information across computer networks.

Root Certificate

A certificate authority (CA) typically exists within a hierarchical structure that contains multiple other CAs with clearly defined parent-child relationships between them. Child or subordinate CAs are certified by their parent CAs, creating a certificate chain. The CA at the top of the hierarchy is referred to as the root CA, and its certificate is called the root certificate. This certificate is typically self-signed.

Secure Sockets Layer (SSL)

Secure Sockets Layer (SSL) and Transport Layer Security (TLS) are cryptographic protocols that provide communication security over a computer network. TLS is the successor of SSL. They both use X.509 certificates to authenticate the server. Both protocols negotiate a symmetric key between the client and the server that is used to encrypt data flowing between the two entities.

Secure HTTPS

HTTPS stands for HTTP over SSL/TLS, a secure form of HTTP that is supported by all major browsers and servers. All HTTP requests and responses are encrypted before being sent across a network. HTTPS combines the HTTP protocol with symmetric, asymmetric, and X.509 certificate-based cryptographic techniques. HTTPS works by inserting a cryptographic security layer below the HTTP application layer and above the TCP transport layer in the Open Systems Interconnection (OSI) model. The security layer uses the Secure Sockets Layer (SSL) protocol or the Transport Layer Security (TLS) protocol.

SSL Server Certificates

HTTPS transactions require server certificates to authenticate a server. A server certificate is an X.509 v3 data structure that binds the public key in the certificate to the subject of the certificate. An SSL/TLS certificate is signed by a certificate authority (CA) and contains the name of the server, the validity period, the public key, the signature algorithm, and more.

Symmetric Key Cryptography

Symmetric key cryptography uses the same key to both encrypt and decrypt digital data. See also Asymmetric Key Cryptography.

Transport Layer Security (TLS)

See Secure Sockets Layer (SSL).

Trust

In order for a web browser to trust the identity of a website, the browser must be able to verify the website's certificate. Browsers, however, trust only a small number of certificates known as CA root certificates. A trusted third party, known as a certificate authority (CA), validates the identity of the website and issues a signed digital certificate to the website's operator. The browser can then check the digital signature to validate the identity of the website. If validation is successful, the browser displays a lock icon in the address bar.

ACM Certificate Characteristics

Certificates provided by ACM have the characteristics described on this page.

Note
These characteristics apply only to certificates provided by ACM. They might not apply to certificates that you import into ACM.

Domain Validation (DV) ACM Certificates are domain validated. That is, the subject field of an ACM Certificate identifies a domain name and nothing more. When you request an ACM Certificate, you must validate that you own or control all of the domains that you specify in your request. You can validate ownership by using email or DNS. For more information, see Use Email to Validate Domain Ownership and Use DNS to Validate Domain Ownership.

Validity Period The validity period for ACM Certificates is currently 13 months.

Managed Renewal and Deployment ACM manages the process of renewing ACM Certificates and provisioning the certificates after they are renewed. Automatic renewal can help you avoid downtime due to incorrectly configured, revoked, or expired certificates. For more information, see Managed Renewal for ACM's Amazon-Issued Certificates.

Browser and Application Trust ACM Certificates are trusted by all major browsers including Google Chrome, Microsoft Internet Explorer and Microsoft Edge, Mozilla Firefox, and Apple Safari. Browsers that trust ACM Certificates display a lock icon in their status bar or address bar when connected by SSL/TLS to sites that use ACM Certificates. ACM Certificates are also trusted by Java.

Multiple Domain Names Each ACM Certificate must include at least one fully qualified domain name (FQDN), and you can add additional names if you want. For example, when you are creating an ACM Certificate for `www.example.com`, you can also add the name `www.example.net` if customers can reach your site by using either name. This is also true of bare domains (also known as the zone apex or naked domains). That is, you can request an ACM Certificate for www.example.com and add the name example.com. For more information, see Request a Public Certificate.

Wildcard Names ACM allows you to use an asterisk (*) in the domain name to create an ACM Certificate containing a wildcard name that can protect several sites in the same domain. For example, `*.example.com` protects `www.example.com` and `images.example.com`.
When you request a wildcard certificate, the asterisk (*) must be in the leftmost position of the domain name and can protect only one subdomain level. For example, ***.example.com** can protect **login.example.com** and **test.example.com**, but it cannot protect **test.login.example.com**. Also note that ***.example.com** protects *only* the subdomains of **example.com**, it does not protect the bare or apex domain (**example.com**). However, you can request a certificate that protects a bare or apex domain and its subdomains by specifying multiple domain names in your request. For example, you can request a certificate that protects **example.com** and ***.example.com**.

Algorithms A certificate must specify an algorithm and key size. Currently, the following public key algorithms are supported by ACM:

- 1024-bit RSA (`RSA_1024`)
- 2048-bit RSA (`RSA_2048`)
- 4096-bit RSA (`RSA_4096`)
- Elliptic Prime Curve 256 bit (`EC_prime256v1`)
- Elliptic Prime Curve 384 bit (`EC_secp384r1`)
- Elliptic Prime Curve 521 bit (`EC_secp521r1`) Note that integrated services allow only algorithms and key sizes they support to be associated with their resources. Further, their support differs depending on whether the certificate is imported into IAM or into ACM. For more information, see the documentation for each service.
- For Elastic Load Balancing, see HTTPS Listeners for Your Application Load Balancer.
- For CloudFront, see Supported SSL/TLS Protocols and Ciphers.

Exceptions Note the following:

- ACM does not provide extended validation (EV) certificates or organization validation (OV) certificates.
- ACM does not provide certificates for anything other than the SSL/TLS protocols.
- You cannot use ACM Certificates for email encryption.
- ACM allows only UTF-8 encoded ASCII for domain names, including labels that contain "xn--" (Punycode). ACM does not accept Unicode input (u-labels) for domain names.
- ACM does not currently permit you to opt out of managed certificate renewal for ACM Certificates. Also, managed renewal is not available for certificates that you import into ACM.
- You cannot request certificates for Amazon-owned domain names such as those ending in amazonaws.com, cloudfront.net, or elasticbeanstalk.com.
- You cannot download the private key for an ACM Certificate.
- You cannot directly install ACM Certificates on your Amazon Elastic Compute Cloud (Amazon EC2) website or application. You can, however, use your certificate with any integrated service. For more information, see Services Integrated with AWS Certificate Manager.

Supported Regions

Visit AWS Regions and Endpoints in the *AWS General Reference* or the AWS Region Table to see the regional availability for ACM.

Like most AWS resources, certificates in ACM are regional resources. To use a certificate with Elastic Load Balancing for the same fully qualified domain name (FQDN) or set of FQDNs in more than one AWS region, you must request or import a certificate for each region. For certificates provided by ACM, this means you must revalidate each domain name in the certificate for each region. You cannot copy a certificate between regions.

To use an ACM Certificate with Amazon CloudFront, you must request or import the certificate in the US East (N. Virginia) region. ACM Certificates in this region that are associated with a CloudFront distribution are distributed to all the geographic locations configured for that distribution.

Services Integrated with AWS Certificate Manager

AWS Certificate Manager supports a growing number of AWS services. You cannot install your ACM certificate or your private ACM PCA certificate directly on your AWS based website or application. You must use one of the following services.

Elastic Load Balancing

Elastic Load Balancing automatically distributes your incoming application traffic across multiple Amazon EC2 instances. It detects unhealthy instances and reroutes traffic to healthy instances until the unhealthy instances have been restored. Elastic Load Balancing automatically scales its request handling capacity in response to incoming traffic. For more information about load balancing, see the Elastic Load Balancing User Guide.

In general, to serve secure content over SSL/TLS, load balancers require that SSL/TLS certificates be installed on either the load balancer or the backend Amazon EC2 instance. ACM is integrated with Elastic Load Balancing to deploy ACM certificates on the load balancer. For more information, see Create an Application Load Balancer.

Amazon CloudFront

Amazon CloudFront is a web service that speeds up distribution of your dynamic and static web content to end users by delivering your content from a worldwide network of edge locations. When an end user requests content that you're serving through CloudFront, the user is routed to the edge location that provides the lowest latency. This ensures that content is delivered with the best possible performance. If the content is currently at that edge location, CloudFront delivers it immediately. If the content is not currently at that edge location, CloudFront retrieves it from the Amazon S3 bucket or web server that you have identified as the definitive content source. For more information about CloudFront, see the Amazon CloudFront Developer Guide.

To serve secure content over SSL/TLS, CloudFront requires that SSL/TLS certificates be installed on either the CloudFront distribution or on the backend content source. ACM is integrated with CloudFront to deploy ACM certificates on the CloudFront distribution. For more information, see Getting an SSL/TLS Certificate.

To use an ACM certificate with CloudFront, you must request or import the certificate in the US East (N. Virginia) region.

AWS Elastic Beanstalk

Elastic Beanstalk helps you deploy and manage applications in the AWS Cloud without worrying about the infrastructure that runs those applications. AWS Elastic Beanstalk reduces management complexity. You simply upload your application and Elastic Beanstalk automatically handles the details of capacity provisioning, load balancing, scaling, and health monitoring. Elastic Beanstalk uses the Elastic Load Balancing service to create a load balancer. For more information about Elastic Beanstalk, see the AWS Elastic Beanstalk Developer Guide. To choose a certificate, you must configure the load balancer for your application in the Elastic Beanstalk console. For more information, see Configuring Your Elastic Beanstalk Environment's Load Balancer to Terminate HTTPS.

Amazon API Gateway

With the proliferation of mobile devices and growth of the Internet of Things (IoT), it has become increasingly common to create APIs that can be used to access data and interact with back-end systems on AWS. You can use API Gateway to publish, maintain, monitor, and secure your APIs. After you deploy your API to API Gateway, you can set up a custom domain name to simplify access to it. To set up a custom domain name, you must provide an SSL/TLS certificate. You can use ACM to generate or import the certificate.

AWS CloudFormation

AWS CloudFormation helps you model and set up your Amazon Web Services resources. You create a template that describes the AWS resources that you want to use, such as Elastic Load Balancing or API Gateway. Then AWS CloudFormation takes care of provisioning and configuring those resources for you. You don't need to individually create and configure AWS resources and figure out what's dependent on what; AWS CloudFormation handles all of that. ACM certificates are included as a template resource, which means that AWS CloudFormation can request ACM certificates that you can use with AWS services to enable secure connections. For more information, see AWS::CertificateManager::Certificate. In addition, ACM certificates are included with many of the AWS resources that you can set up with AWS CloudFormation.

If you create an ACM certificate with AWS CloudFormation, the AWS CloudFormation stack remains in the **CREATE_IN_PROGRESS** state. Any further stack operations are delayed until you act upon the instructions in the certificate validation email. For more information, see Resource Failed to Stabilize During a Create, Update, or Delete Stack Operation.

Site Seals and Trust Logos

Amazon doesn't provide a site seal or allow its trademark to be used as one:

- AWS Certificate Manager (ACM) doesn't provide a secure site seal that you can use on your website. If you want to use a site seal, you can obtain one from a third-party vendor. We recommend choosing a vendor that evaluates and asserts the security of your website or business practices.
- Amazon doesn't allow its trademark or logo to be used as a certificate badge, site seal, or trust logo. Seals and badges of this type can be copied to sites that don't use the ACM service, and can be used inappropriately to establish trust under false pretenses. To protect our customers and the reputation of Amazon, we don't allow our trademark and logo to be used in this way.

Limits

The following AWS Certificate Manager (ACM) limits apply to each AWS region and each AWS account. To request higher limits, create a case at the AWS Support Center. New AWS accounts might start with limits that are lower than those that are described here.

Item	Default Limit
Number of ACM Certificates	100
Number of ACM Certificates per Year (last 365 days)	Twice your account limit
Number of imported certificates	100
Number of imported certificates per year (last 365 days)	Twice your account limit
Number of Domain Names per ACM Certificate	10
Number of Private CAs	10
Number of Private Certificates per CA	50,000

Topics

- Number of ACM Certificates per Year (Last 365 Days)
- Number of Domain Names per ACM Certificate
- Number of Private CAs and Certificates

Number of ACM Certificates per Year (Last 365 Days)

You can request up to twice your limit of ACM Certificates every year. For example, if your limit is 25, you can request up to 50 ACM Certificates a year. If you request 50 certificates, you must delete 25 during the year to stay within your limit. If you need more than 25 certificates, in this example, you must contact the **AWS Support Center**.

Note
Although the preceding table indicates that an account can own up to 100 ACM Certificates, new AWS accounts might start with a lower limit.

Number of Domain Names per ACM Certificate

The default limit is 10 domain names for each ACM Certificate. Your limit may be greater. The first domain name that you submit is included as the subject common name (CN) of the certificate. All names are included in the Subject Alternative Name extension.

You can request up to 100 domain names. To request an increase in your limit, create a case at the AWS Support Center . Before creating a case, however, make sure you understand how adding more domain names can create more administrative work for you if you use email validation. For more information, see Domain Validation.

Note
The limit for the number of domain names per ACM Certificate applies only to certificates that are provided by ACM. This limit does not apply to certificates that you import into ACM. The following sections apply only to ACM Certificates.

Number of Private CAs and Certificates

ACM is integrated with ACM PCA. You can use the ACM console, AWS CLI, or ACM API to request private certificates from an existing private certificate authority (CA). The certificates are managed within the ACM environment and have the same restrictions as public certificates issued by ACM. For more information, see Request a Private Certificate. You can also issue private certificates by using the standalone ACM PCA service. For more information, see Issue a Private Certificate. You can create 10 private CAs and 50,000 private certificates for each.

Best Practices

Best practices are recommendations that can help you use AWS Certificate Manager (AWS Certificate Manager) more effectively. The following best practices are based on real-world experience from current ACM customers.

Topics

- AWS CloudFormation
- Certificate Pinning
- Domain Validation
- Adding or Deleting Domain Names
- Opting Out of Certificate Transparency Logging
- Turn on AWS CloudTrail

AWS CloudFormation

With AWS CloudFormation you can create a template that describes the AWS resources that you want to use. AWS CloudFormation then provisions and configures those resources for you. AWS CloudFormation can provision resources that are supported by ACM such as Elastic Load Balancing, Amazon CloudFront, and Amazon API Gateway. For more information, see Services Integrated with AWS Certificate Manager.

If you use AWS CloudFormation to quickly create and delete multiple test environments, we recommend that you do not create a separate ACM Certificate for each environment. Doing so will quickly exhaust your certificate limit. For more information, see Limits. Instead, create a wildcard certificate that covers all of the domain names that you are using for testing. For example, if you repeatedly create ACM Certificates for domain names that vary by only a version number, such as `.service.example.com`, create instead a single wildcard certificate for `<*>.service.example.com`. Include the wildcard certificate in the template that AWS CloudFormation uses to create your test environment.

Certificate Pinning

Certificate pinning, sometimes known as SSL pinning, is a process that you can use in your application to validate a remote host by associating that host directly with its X.509 certificate or public key instead of with a certificate hierarchy. The application therefore uses pinning to bypass SSL/TLS certificate chain validation. The typical SSL validation process checks signatures throughout the certificate chain from the root certificate authority (CA) certificate through the subordinate CA certificates, if any. It also checks the certificate for the remote host at the bottom of the hierarchy. Your application can instead pin to the certificate for the remote host to say that *only that* certificate and not the root certificate or any other in the chain is trusted. You can add the remote host's certificate or public key to your application during development. Alternatively, the application can add the certificate or key when it first connects to the host.

Warning
We recommend that your application **not** pin an ACM Certificate. ACM performs Managed Renewal for ACM's Amazon-Issued Certificates to automatically renew your Amazon-issued SSL/TLS certificates before they expire. To renew a certificate, ACM generates a new public-private key pair. If your application pins the ACM Certificate and the certificate is successfully renewed with a new public key, the application might be unable to connect to your domain.

If you decide to pin a certificate, the following options will not hinder your application from connecting to your domain:

- Import your own certificate into ACM and then pin your application to the imported certificate. ACM doesn't try to automatically renew imported certificates.
- Pin your application to an Amazon root certificate.

Domain Validation

Before the Amazon certificate authority (CA) can issue a certificate for your site, AWS Certificate Manager (ACM) must verify that you own or control all the domains that you specified in your request. You can perform verification using either email or DNS. For more information, see Use Email to Validate Domain Ownership and Use DNS to Validate Domain Ownership.

Adding or Deleting Domain Names

You cannot add or remove domain names from an existing ACM Certificate. Instead you must request a new certificate with the revised list of domain names. For example, if your certificate has five domain names and you want to add four more, you must request a new certificate with all nine domain names. As with any new certificate, you must validate ownership of all the domain names in the request, including the names that you previously validated for the original certificate.

If you use email validation, you receive up to 8 validation email messages for each domain, at least 1 of which must be acted upon within 72 hours. For example, when you request a certificate with five domain names, you receive up to 40 validation messages, at least 5 of which must be acted upon within 72 hours. As the number of domain names in the certificate request increases, so does the work required to use email to validate domain ownership.

If you use DNS validation instead, you must write one new DNS record to the database for the FQDN you want to validate. ACM sends you the record to create and later queries the database to determine whether the record has been added. Adding the record asserts that you own or control the domain. In the preceding example, if you request a certificate with five domain names, you must create five DNS records. We recommend that you use DNS validation when possible.

Opting Out of Certificate Transparency Logging

Important
Regardless of the actions you take to opt out of certificate transparency logging, your certificate might still be logged by any client or individual that has access to the public or private endpoint to which you bind the certificate. However, the certificate won't contain a signed certificate timestamp (SCT). Only the issuing CA can embed an SCT in a certificate.

Beginning April 30 2018, Google Chrome will stop trusting public SSL/TLS certificates that are not recorded in a certificate transparency log. Therefore, beginning April 24 2018, the Amazon CA will start publishing all new certificates and renewals to at least two public logs. Once a certificate has been logged, it cannot be removed. For more information, see Certificate Transparency Logging.

Logging is performed automatically when you request a certificate or when a certificate is renewed, but you can choose to opt out. Common reasons for doing so include concerns about security and privacy. For example, logging internal host domain names gives potential attackers information about internal networks that would otherwise not be public. In addition, logging could leak the names of new or unreleased products and websites.

To opt out of transparency logging when you are requesting a certificate, use the **Options** parameter of the request-certificate AWS CLI command or the RequestCertificate API.

If your certificate was issued before April 24 2018 and you want to make sure that it is not logged during renewal, you can call the `update-certificate-options` command or the UpdateCertificateOptions API to opt out.

Once a certificate has been logged, it cannot be removed from the log. Opting out at that point will have no effect. If you opt out of logging when you request a certificate and then choose later to opt back in, your certificate will not be logged until it is renewed. If you want the certificate to be logged immediately, we recommend that you issue a new one.

Note

You cannot currently use the console to opt out of or in to transparency logging.

The following example shows you how to use the request-certificate command to disable certificate transparency when you request a new certificate.

```
1 aws acm request-certificate \
2 --domain-name www.example.com \
3 --validation-method DNS \
4 --options CertificateTransparencyLoggingPreference=DISABLED \
5 --idempotency-token 184627
```

The preceding command outputs the ARN of your new certificate.

```
1 {
2     "CertificateArn": "arn:aws:acm:region:account:certificate
          /12345678-1234-1234-1234-123456789012"
3 }
```

If you already have a certificate, and you don't want it to be logged when it is renewed, use the update-certificate-options command. This command does not return a value.

```
1 aws acm update-certificate-options \
2 --certificate-arn arn:aws:acm:region:account:\
3 certificate/12345678-1234-1234-1234-123456789012 \
4 --options CertificateTransparencyLoggingPreference=DISABLED
```

Turn on AWS CloudTrail

Turn on CloudTrail logging before you begin using ACM. CloudTrail enables you to monitor your AWS deployments by retrieving a history of AWS API calls for your account, including API calls made via the AWS Management Console, the AWS SDKs, the AWS Command Line Interface, and higher-level AWS services. You can also identify which users and accounts called the ACM APIs, the source IP address the calls were made from, and when the calls occurred. You can integrate CloudTrail into applications using the API, automate trail creation for your organization, check the status of your trails, and control how administrators turn CloudTrail logging on and off. For more information, see Creating a Trail. Go to Using AWS CloudTrail to see example trails for ACM actions.

Pricing for AWS Certificate Manager

You are not charged by AWS for the SSL/TLS certificates that you manage with AWS Certificate Manager. You pay only for the AWS resources that you create to run your website or application. For the latest ACM pricing information, see the AWS Certificate Manager Service Pricing page on the AWS website.

Setting Up

With AWS Certificate Manager (ACM) you can provision and manage SSL/TLS certificates for your AWS based websites and applications. You use ACM to create or import and then manage a certificate. You must use other AWS services to deploy the certificate to your website or application. For more information about the services integrated with ACM, see Services Integrated with AWS Certificate Manager. The following topics discuss the steps you need to perform before using ACM.

Note
In addition to using certificates provided by ACM, you can also import certificates into ACM. For more information, see Importing Certificates.

Topics

- Set Up AWS and IAM
- Register a Domain Name
- Set Up Your Website or Application
- (Optional) Configure Email for Your Domain
- (Optional) Configure a CAA Record

Set Up AWS and IAM

Before you can use ACM, you must sign up for Amazon Web Services. As a best practice, you can create an IAM user to limit the actions your users can perform.

Sign Up for AWS

If you are not already an Amazon Web Services (AWS) customer, you must sign up to be able to use ACM. Your account is automatically signed up for all available services, but you are charged for only the services that you use. Also, if you are a new AWS customer, you can get started for free. For more information, see AWS Free Tier.

To sign up for an AWS account

1. Go to https://aws.amazon.com/ and choose **Sign Up**.

2. Follow the on-screen instructions.

Note
Part of the sign-up procedure includes receiving an automated telephone call and entering the supplied PIN on the telephone keypad. You must also supply a credit card number even if you are signing up for the free tier.

Create an IAM User

All AWS accounts have root user credentials (that is, the credentials of the account owner). These credentials allow full access to all resources in the account. Because you can't restrict permissions for root user credentials, we recommend that you delete your root user access keys. Then create AWS Identity and Access Management (IAM) user credentials for everyday interaction with AWS. For more information, see Lock away your AWS account (root) access keys in the *IAM User Guide*.

Note
You may need AWS account root user access for specific tasks, such as changing an AWS support plan or closing your account. In these cases, sign in to the AWS Management Console with your email and password. See Email and Password (Root User).

For a list of tasks that require root user access, see AWS Tasks That Require AWS Account Root User.

With IAM, you can securely control access to AWS services and resources for users in your AWS account. For example, if you require administrator-level permissions, you can create an IAM user, grant that user full access, and then use those credentials to interact with AWS. If you need to modify or revoke your permissions, you can delete or modify the policies that are associated with that IAM user.

If you have multiple users that require access to your AWS account, you can create unique credentials for each user and define who has access to which resources. You don't need to share credentials. For example, you can create IAM users with read-only access to resources in your AWS account and distribute those credentials to your users.

ACM also provides two AWS managed policies that you can use:

- **AWSCertificateManagerFullAccess**
- **AWSCertificateManagerReadOnly**

Note
Any activity or costs that are associated with the IAM user are billed to the AWS account owner.

Register a Domain Name

A fully qualified domain name (FQDN) is the unique name of an organization or individual on the Internet followed by a top-level domain extension such as .com or .org. If you do not already have a registered domain name, you can register one through Amazon Route 53 or dozens of other commercial registrars. Typically you go to the registrar's website and request a domain name. The registrar queries WHOIS to determine whether the requested FQDN is available. If it is, the registrar usually lists related names that differ by domain extension and provides you an opportunity to acquire any of the available names. Registration usually lasts for a set period of time such as one or two years before it must be renewed.

For more information about registering domain names with Amazon Route 53, see Registering Domain Names Using Amazon Route 53 in the *Amazon Route 53 Developer Guide*.

Set Up Your Website or Application

You can install your website on an Amazon EC2 Linux or Windows instance. For more information about Linux Amazon EC2 instances, see Amazon Elastic Compute Cloud User Guide for Linux. For more information about Windows Amazon EC2 instances, see Amazon Elastic Compute Cloud User Guide for Microsoft Windows.

Although you install your website on an Amazon EC2 instance, you cannot directly deploy an ACM Certificate on that instance. You must instead deploy your certificate by using one of the services integrated with ACM. For more information see Services Integrated with AWS Certificate Manager.

To get your website up and running quickly on either Windows or Linux, see the following topics.

Topics

- Linux Quickstart
- Windows Quickstart

Linux Quickstart

To create your website or application on a Linux instance, you can choose a Linux Amazon Machine Image (AMI) and install an Apache web server on it. For more information, see Tutorial: Installing a LAMP Web Server on Amazon Linux in the *Amazon EC2 User Guide for Linux Instances*.

Windows Quickstart

To acquire a Microsoft Windows server on which you can install your website or application, choose a Windows Server AMI that comes bundled with a Microsoft Internet Information Services (IIS) web server. Then use the default website or create a new one. You can also install a WIMP server on your Amazon EC2 instance. For more information, see Tutorial: Installing a WIMP Server on an Amazon EC2 Instance Running Windows Server in the *Amazon EC2 User Guide for Windows Instances*.

(Optional) Configure Email for Your Domain

Note
The following steps are required only if you use email validation to assert that you own or control the FQDN (fully qualified domain name) specified in your certificate request. ACM requires that you validate ownership or control before it issues a certificate. You can use either email validation or DNS validation. For more information about email validation, see Use Email to Validate Domain Ownership.

If you are able to edit your DNS configuration, we recommend that you use DNS domain validation rather than email validation. DNS validation removes the need to configure email for the domain name. For more information about DNS validation, see Use DNS to Validate Domain Ownership.

Use your registrar's website to associate your contact addresses with your domain name. The registrar adds the contact email addresses to the WHOIS database and adds one or more mail servers to the mail exchanger (MX) records of a DNS server. If you choose to use email validation, ACM sends email to the contact addresses and to five common administrative addresses formed from your MX record. ACM sends up to eight validation email messages every time you create a new certificate, renew a certificate, or request new validation mail. The validation email contains instructions for confirming that the domain owner or an appointed representative approves the ACM Certificate. For more information, see Use Email to Validate Domain Ownership. If you have trouble with validation email, see Troubleshoot Email Problems.

WHOIS Database

The WHOIS database contains contact information for your domain. To validate your identity, ACM sends an email to the following three addresses in WHOIS. You must make sure that your contact information is public or that email that is sent to an obfuscated address is forwarded to your real email address.

- Domain registrant
- Technical contact
- Administrative contact

MX Record

When you register your domain, your registrar sends your mail exchanger (MX) record to a Domain Name System (DNS) server. An MX record indicates which servers accept mail for your domain. The record contains a fully qualified domain name (FQDN). You can request a certificate for apex domains or subdomains.

For example, if you use the console to request a certificate for abc.xyz.example.com, ACM first tries to find the MX record for that subdomain. If that record cannot be found, ACM performs an MX lookup for xyz.example.com. If that record cannot be found, ACM performs an MX lookup for example.com. If that record cannot be found or there is no MX record, ACM chooses the original domain for which the certificate was requested (abc.xyz.example.com in this example). ACM then sends email to the following five common system administration addresses for the domain or subdomain:

- administrator@*your_domain_name*
- hostmaster@*your_domain_name*
- postmaster@*your_domain_name*
- webmaster@*your_domain_name*
- admin@*your_domain_name*

If you are using the RequestCertificate API operation or the request-certificate AWS CLI command, AWS does not perform an MX lookup. Instead, `RequestCertificate` lets you specify both your domain name and the name of a validation domain. If you specify the optional `ValidationDomain` parameter, AWS sends the preceding five email messages there rather than to your domain.

ACM always sends validation email to the five common addresses listed previously whether you are using the console, the API, or the AWS CLI. However, AWS performs an MX lookup only when you use the console to request a certificate.

If you do not receive validation email, see Not Receiving Validation Email for information about possible causes and workarounds.

(Optional) Configure a CAA Record

You can optionally configure a Certification Authority Authorization (CAA) DNS record to specify that AWS Certificate Manager (ACM) is allowed to issue a certificate for your domain or subdomain. After it validates your domain, ACM checks for the presence of CAA records to make sure it can issue a certificate for you. You can choose to not configure a CAA record for your domain or leave the record blank if you do not want to enable CAA checking. A CAA record contains the following data fields:

flags
Specifies whether the value of the **tag** field is supported by ACM. Set this value to **0**.

tag
The **tag** field can be one of the following values. Note that the **iodef** field is currently ignored.
issue
Indicates that the ACM CA that you specify in the **value** field is authorized to issue a certificate for your domain or subdomain.
issuewild
Indicates that the ACM CA that you specified in the **value** field is authorized to issue a wildcard certificate for your domain or subdomain. A wildcard certificate applies to the domain or subdomain and all of its subdomains.

value
The value of this field depends on the value of the **tag** field. You must enclose this value in quotation marks (""").
When **tag** is **issue**
The **value** field contains the CA domain name. This field can contain the name of a CA other than an Amazon CA. However, if you do not have a CAA record that specifies one of the following four Amazon CAs, ACM cannot issue a certificate to your domain or subdomain:

- amazon.com
- amazontrust.com
- awstrust.com
- amazonaws.com The **value** field can also contain a semicolon (;) to indicate that no CA should be permitted to issue a certificate for your domain or subdomain. Use this field if you decide at some point that you no longer want a certificate issued for a particular domain.
  When **tag** is **issuewild**
  The **value** field is the same as that for when **tag** is **issue** except that the value applies to wildcard certificates.

Example CAA Record Examples
In the following examples, your domain name comes first followed by the record type (CAA). The **flags** field is always 0. The **tags** field can be **issue** or **issuewild**. If the field is **issue** and you type the domain name of a CA server in the **value** field, the CAA record indicates that your specified server is permitted to issue your requested certificate. If you type a semicolon ";" in the **value** field, the CAA record indicates that no CA is permitted to issue a certificate. The configuration of CAA records varies by DNS provider.

```
1 Domain      Record type  Flags  Tag      Value
2
3 example.com.  CAA            0    issue    "SomeCA.com"
4 example.com.  CAA            0    issue    "amazon.com"
5 example.com.  CAA            0    issue    "amazontrust.com"
6 example.com.  CAA            0    issue    "awstrust.com"
7 example.com.  CAA            0    issue    "amazonaws.com"
8 example.com   CAA            0    issue    ";"
```

For more information about how to add or modify DNS records, check with your DNS provider. Route 53 supports CAA records. If Route 53 is your DNS provider, see CAA Format for more information about creating a record.

Getting Started

Sign into the AWS Management Console and open the ACM console at https://console.aws.amazon.com/acm/home. If the introductory page appears, choose **Get Started**. Otherwise, choose **Certificate Manager** or **Private CAs** in the left navigation pane.

ACM supports SSL/TLS certificates that can be used to enable secure communication across the internet or over an internal network. You can request a publicly trusted certificate issued by ACM or import a certificate. Imported certificates can be issued by a third party and publicly trusted, or they can be self-signed. You can also use the ACM console to request that a private certificate be issued by a private certificate authority (CA) in your organization. Private certificates are not trusted by default. Administrators must install them in client trust stores.

This documentation primarily discusses public ACM and third party certificates. It also discusses how to issue a private certificate using an existing private CA. To learn more about creating and using a private CA, see AWS Certificate Manager Private Certificate Authority.

Topics

- Request a Public Certificate
- Request a Private Certificate
- Export a Private Certificate
- Use DNS to Validate Domain Ownership
- Use Email to Validate Domain Ownership
- List ACM–Managed Certificates
- Describe ACM Certificates
- Delete ACM–Managed Certificates
- Install ACM Certificates
- Resend Validation Email (Optional)

Request a Public Certificate

The following sections discuss how to use the ACM console or AWS CLI to request a public ACM certificate. If you are having trouble requesting a certificate, see Troubleshoot Certificate Request Problems. If you are having trouble requesting a certificate for an .IO domain, see Troubleshoot .IO Domain Problems. To request a private certificate using your private certificate authority (CA), see Request a Private Certificate.

Topics

- Requesting a public certificate using the console
- Requesting a public certificate using the CLI

Requesting a public certificate using the console

To request an ACM public certificate (console)

1. Sign into the AWS Management Console and open the ACM console at https://console.aws.amazon.com/acm/home.

2. On the **Request a certificate** page, type your domain name. You can use a fully qualified domain name (FQDN) such as **www.example.com** or a bare or apex domain name such as **example.com**. You can also use an asterisk (*****) as a wildcard in the leftmost position to protect several site names in the same domain. For example, ***.example.com** protects **corp.example.com**, and **images.example.com**. The wildcard name will appear in the **Subject** field and the **Subject Alternative Name** extension of the ACM certificate. **Note**
   When you request a wildcard certificate, the asterisk (*****) must be in the leftmost position of the domain name and can protect only one subdomain level. For example, ***.example.com** can protect **login.example.com**, and **test.example.com**, but it cannot protect **test.login.example.com**. Also note that ***.example.com** protects *only* the subdomains of **example.com**, it does not protect the bare or apex domain (**example.com**). To protect both, see the next step.

3. To add more domain names to the ACM certificate, choose **Add more names** and type another domain name in the text box that opens. This is useful for protecting both a bare or apex domain (like **example.com**) and its subdomains (***.example.com**).

4. After you have typed valid domain names, choose **Review and Request** or choose **Cancel** to quit. **Important**
   Unless you choose to opt out, your certificate will be automatically recorded in at least two public certificate transparency databases. You cannot currently use the console to opt out. You must use the AWS CLI or the API. For more information, see Opting Out of Certificate Transparency Logging. For general information about transparency logs, see Certificate Transparency Logging.

5. If the review page correctly contains the information that you provided for your request, choose **Confirm and request**. The following page shows that your request status is pending validation.

Before ACM issues a certificate, it validates that you own or control the domain names in your certificate request. You can use either email validation or DNS validation. If you choose email validation, ACM sends validation email to three contact addresses registered in the WHOIS database and to five common system administration addresses for each domain name. You or an authorized representative must reply to one of

these email messages. For more information, see Use Email to Validate Domain Ownership. If you use DNS validation, you simply write a CNAME record provided by ACM to your DNS configuration. For more information about DNS validation, see Use DNS to Validate Domain Ownership. **Note**
If you are able to edit your DNS configuration, we recommend that you use DNS domain validation rather than email validation. DNS validation has multiple benefits over email validation. See Use DNS to Validate Domain Ownership.

Requesting a public certificate using the CLI

Use the request-certificate command to request a new public ACM certificate on the command line.

```
1 aws acm request-certificate \
2 --domain-name www.example.com \
3 --validation-method DNS \
4 --idempotency-token 1234 \
5 --options CertificateTransparencyLoggingPreference=DISABLED
```

This command outputs the Amazon Resource Name (ARN) of your new private certificate.

```
1 {
2     "CertificateArn": "arn:aws:acm:region:account:certificate
          /12345678-1234-1234-1234-123456789012"
3 }
```

Request a Private Certificate

The following sections discuss how to use the ACM console or the ACM PCA CLI request a private certificate from an existing private certificate authority (CA). For more information about creating a private CA, see Create a Private Certificate Authority.

Private certificates issued by ACM resemble public certificates issued by ACM. The certificates have the following restrictions:

- You must use DNS subject names. For more information, see Domain Names
- You can use only a 2048 bit RSA private key algorithm.
- The only supported signing algorithm is SHA256WithRSAEncryption.
- Each certificate is valid for 13 months.
- The private CA must be Active, and the CA private key type must be RSA 2048 or RSA 4096.
- ACM renews the certificate automatically, if possible, after 11 months.

Private certificates issued by ACM PCA do not have the preceding restrictions. You can use your private CA to create certificates that have any subject name, use any of the supported private key algorithms, any signing algorithm, and any validity period. This is beneficial if you must identify a subject by a specific name or if you cannot rotate certificates easily. For more information, see Issue a Private Certificate.

Topics

- Requesting a private certificate using the console
- Requesting a private certificate using the CLI

Requesting a private certificate using the console

1. Sign into the AWS Management Console and open the ACM console at https://console.aws.amazon.com/acm/home.

2. Select **Request a private certificate** and then choose **Request a certificate**.

3. Select your private CA from the dropdown list. Information about the CA is filled in below the list to help you verify that you have chosen the CA you want. **Note**
   The ACM console displays **Ineligible** for private CAs with ECDSA keys.

4. Choose **Next**.

5. On the **Request a certificate** page, type a domain name. You can use a fully qualified domain name (FQDN) such as **www.example.com** or a bare or apex domain name such as **example.com**. You can also use an asterisk (*****) as a wildcard in the leftmost position to protect several site names in the same domain. For example, ***.example.com** protects **corp.example.com**, and **images.example.com**. The wildcard name will appear in the **Subject** field and the **Subject Alternative Name** extension of the ACM certificate. **Note**
   When you request a wildcard certificate, the asterisk (*****) must be in the leftmost position of the domain name and can protect only one subdomain level. For example, ***.example.com** can protect **login.example.com**, and **test.example.com**, but it cannot protect **test.login.example.com**. Also note that ***.example.com** protects *only* the subdomains of **example.com**, it does not protect the bare or apex domain (**example.com**). To protect both, see the next step.

6. To add more domain names to the ACM certificate, choose **Add more names** and type another domain name in the text box that opens. This is useful for protecting both a bare or apex domain (like **example.com**) and its subdomains (***.example.com**).

7. After you have typed valid names, choose **Review and Request** or choose **Cancel** to quit.

8. Check the review page to make sure that everything is correct and then choose **Confirm and request**.
   Note
   You do not need to validate a private certificate.

Requesting a private certificate using the CLI

Use the request-certificate command to request a private certificate in ACM.

```
1 aws acm request-certificate \
2 --domain-name www.example.com \
3 --idempotency-token 12563 \
4 --options CertificateTransparencyLoggingPreference=DISABLED \
5 --certificate-authority-arn arn:aws:acm-pca:region:account:\
6 certificate-authority/12345678-1`234-1234-1234-123456789012
```

This command outputs the Amazon Resource Name (ARN) of your new private certificate.

```
1 {
2     "CertificateArn": "arn:aws:acm:region:account:certificate
          /12345678-1234-1234-1234-123456789012"
3 }
```

Export a Private Certificate

You can export a private certificate for use anywhere. You can export the certificate, the certificate chain, and the encrypted private key. You must store the private key securely. The key is related to the public key that is embedded in the certificate.

The private key is a 2048 bit RSA key. You can use the following OpenSSL command to decrypt it. Provide the passphrase when prompted.

```
1 openssl rsa -in encrypted_key.pem -out decrypted_key.pem
```

Topics

- Exporting a private certificate using the console
- Exporting a private certificate using the CLI

Exporting a private certificate using the console

1. Sign into the AWS Management Console and open the ACM console at https://console.aws.amazon.com/acm/home.

2. Choose **Certificate Manager**

3. Select the certificate that you want to export.

4. On the **Actions** menu, choose **Export (private certificates only)**.

5. Enter and confirm a passphrase for the private key.

6. Choose **Generate PEM Encoding**.

7. You can copy the certificate, certificate chain, and encrypted key to memory or choose **Export to a file ** for each.

8. Choose **Done**.

Exporting a private certificate using the CLI

Use the export-certificate command to export a private certificate and private key. For added security, store your passphrase securely in a file before using this command. This prevents your passphrase from being stored in command history and prevents others from seeing the passphrase as you type it in.

```
1 aws acm export-certificate --certificate-arn \
2 arn:aws:acm:rogion:account:\
3 certificate/12345678-1234-1234-1234-123456789012 \
4 --passphrase --file://path-to-passphrase-file
```

This command outputs the base64-encoded, PEM format certificate, the certificate chain, and private key.

```
1 {
2     "PrivateKey":
3        "-----BEGIN ENCRYPTED PRIVATE KEY-----
4         ...Base64-encoded private key ...
5        -----END ENCRYPTED PRIVATE KEY-----",
6     "CertificateChain":
7        "-----BEGIN CERTIFICATE-----
8         ...Base64-encoded certificate...
9        -----END CERTIFICATE-----
```

```
10        ...Base64-encoded certificate...
11        -----BEGIN CERTIFICATE-----
12        ...Base64-encoded private key...
13        -----END CERTIFICATE-----",
14    "Certificate":
15     "-----BEGIN CERTIFICATE-----
16        ...Base64-encoded certificate...
17        -----END CERTIFICATE-----"
18 }
```

Use DNS to Validate Domain Ownership

Before the Amazon certificate authority (CA) can issue a certificate for your site, AWS Certificate Manager (ACM) must verify that you own or control all of the domain names that you specified in your request. You can choose either email validation or DNS validation when you request a certificate. This topic discusses DNS validation. For information about email validation, see Use Email to Validate Domain Ownership.

Note
Validation applies only to certificates provided by AWS Certificate Manager (ACM). ACM does not validate domain ownership for imported certificates.

The Domain Name System (DNS) is a directory service for resources connected to a network. On the internet, DNS servers are used primarily to translate from domain names to the numerical IP addresses that identify and locate resources such as computers and other devices. The databases on DNS servers contain domain records that are used for this translation and to enable other functionality. For example, A records are a type of DNS record used to map domain names to IPV4 addresses. MX records are used to route email. NS records list all of the name servers for the domain.

ACM uses CNAME (Canonical Name) records to validate that you own or control a domain. When you choose DNS validation, ACM provides you one or more CNAME records to insert into your DNS database. For example, if you request a certificate for the `example.com` domain with `www.example.com` as an additional name, ACM creates two CNAME records for you. Each record, created specifically for your domain and your account, contains a name and a value. The value is an alias that points to a domain that ACM owns and which ACM uses to automatically renew your certificate. You add the CNAME records to your DNS database only once. ACM automatically renews your certificate as long as the certificate is in use and your CNAME record remains in place. In addition, if you use Amazon Route 53 to create your domain, ACM can write the CNAME records for you.

The following table shows example CNAME records for five domain names. The $\_x$ values are long random strings generated by ACM. For example `_3639ac514e785e898d2646601fa951d5.example.com` is representative of a generated name. Note that the first two $\_x$ values in the table are the same. That is, the random string created by ACM for the wildcard name `*.example.com` is the same as that created for the base domain name `example.com`. Note also that ACM creates different CNAME records for `example.com` and `www.example.com`.

If you see an expand arrow () in the upper-right corner of the table, you can open the table in a new window. To close the window, choose the close button (**X**) in the lower-right corner.

Domain name	DNS zone	Name	Type	Value
*.example.com	example.com	_x1.example.com	CNAME	_x2.acm-validations.aws
example.com	example.com	_x1.example.com	CNAME	_x2.acm-validations.aws
www.example.com	example.com	_x3.www.example.com	CNAME	_x4.acm-validations.aws
host.example.com	example.com	_x5.host.example.com	CNAME	_x6.acm-validations.aws
subdomain.example.com	subdomain.example.com	_x7.subdomain.example.com	CNAME	_x8.acm-validations.aws
host.subdomain.example.com	subdomain.example.com	_x9.host.subdomain.example.com	CNAME	_x10.acm-validations.aws

DNS validation has a number of advantages over email validation:

- DNS requires that you create only one CNAME record per domain name when you request an ACM Certificate. Email validation sends up to eight email messages per domain name.
- You can request additional ACM Certificates for your FQDN for as long as the DNS record remains in place. That is, you can create multiple certificates that have the same domain name. You do not need to get a new CNAME record. There are many reasons to do this. You might, for example, want new certificates that cover different subdomains. You might want to create the same certificate in multiple regions (the validation token works for any region). You might want to replace a certificate that you deleted.
- ACM automatically renews ACM Certificates that you validated by using DNS. ACM renews each certificate before it expires as long as the certificate is in use and the DNS record is in place.
- ACM can add the CNAME record for you if you use Route 53 to manage your public DNS records.
- You can more easily automate the DNS validation process than you can the email validation process.

Note however that you may be required to use email validation if you do not have permission to modify the DNS records for your domain.

To use DNS validation:

1. Sign into the AWS Management Console and open the ACM console at https://console.aws.amazon. com/acm/home. If the introductory page appears, choose **Get Started**. Otherwise, choose **Request a certificate**.

2. On the **Request a certificate** page, type your domain name. For more information about typing domain names, see Request a Public Certificate.

3. To add more domain names to the ACM Certificate, type other names as text boxes open beneath the name you just typed.

4. Choose **Next**.

5. Choose **DNS validation**.

6. Choose **Review and request**. Verify that the domain name and validation method are correct.

7. Choose **Confirm and request**.

8. On the **Validation** page, expand your domain information or choose **Export DNS configuration to a file**. If you expand your domain information, ACM displays the name and value of the CNAME record you must add to your DNS database to validate that you control the domain.

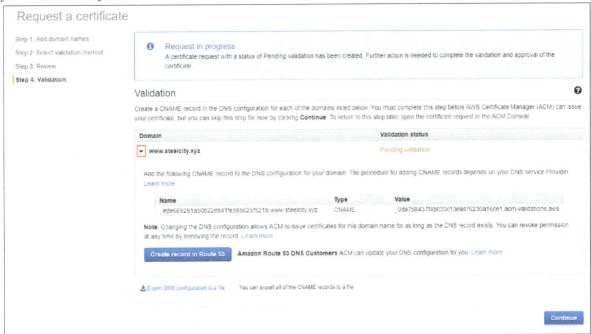

9. The **Create record in Route 53** button appears if the following conditions are true:

   - You use Route 53 as your DNS provider.
   - You are hosting the domain in Route 53.
   - You have permission to write to the Route 53, hosted zone.
   - Your FQDN has not already been validated.

If your FQDN has already been validated or if you don't have permission to write to the Route 53 hosted zone for the domain name you are requesting, the **Create record in Route 53** button will appear disabled. For more information about Route 53 record sets, see Working with Resource Record Sets. **Note** Currently, you cannot programmatically request that ACM automatically create your record in Route 53. You can, however, make a AWS CLI or API call to Route 53 to create the record.

10. Add the record from the console or the exported file to your database. For more information about adding DNS records, see Adding a CNAME to Your Database. You can choose **Continue** to skip this step. You can return to it later by opening the certificate request in the console. **Note**

    If your FQDN was validated when you requested a previous certificate and you are requesting another certificate for the same FQDN, you do not need to add another DNS record. **Note**

    Adding a CNAME record that contains a domain name (such as *.example.com*) might result in duplication of the domain name (such as *.example.com.example.com*). To avoid duplication, you can manually copy only the part of the CNAME that you need. This would be of the form *_3639ac514e785e898d2646601fa951d5*.

11. After updating your DNS configuration, choose **Continue**. ACM displays a table view that includes all of your certificates. The certificate you requested and its status is displayed. After your DNS provider propagates your record update, it can take up to several hours for ACM to validate the domain name and issue the certificate. During this time, ACM shows the validation status as **Pending validation**. After validating the domain name, ACM changes the validation status to **Success**. After AWS issues the certificate, ACM changes the certificate status to **Issued**. **Note**

    If ACM is not able to validate the domain name within 72 hours from the time it generates a CNAME value for you, ACM changes the certificate status to **Validation timed out**. The most likely reason for this result is that you did not update your DNS configuration with the value that ACM generated. To remedy this issue, you must request a new certificate.

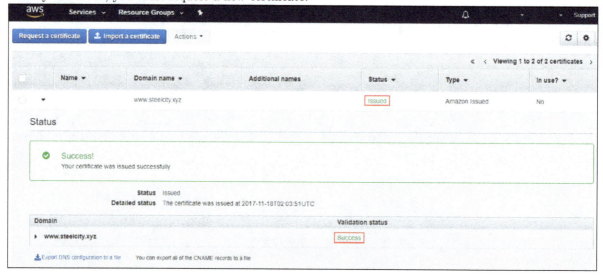

Adding a CNAME to Your Database

To use DNS validation, you must be able to add a CNAME record to the DNS configuration for your domain. If Route 53 is not your DNS provider, contact your provider to find out how to add records. If Route 53 is your provider, ACM can create the CNAME record for you as discussed previously in step 9. If you want to add the record yourself, see Editing Resource Record Sets in the *Route 53 Developer Guide*.

Note
If you do not have permission to edit your DNS configuration, you must use email validation.

Deleting a CNAME from Your Database

ACM automatically renews your certificate for as long as the certificate is in use and the CNAME record that ACM created for you remains in place in your DNS database. You can stop automatic renewal by removing the certificate from the AWS service with which it is associated or by deleting the CNAME record. If Route 53 is not your DNS provider, contact your provider to find out how to delete the record. If Route 53 is your provider, see Deleting Resource Record Sets in the *Route 53 Developer Guide*. For more information about managed certificate renewal, see Managed Renewal for ACM's Amazon-Issued Certificates.

Use Email to Validate Domain Ownership

Before the Amazon certificate authority (CA) can issue a certificate for your site, AWS Certificate Manager (ACM) must verify that you own or control all of the domains that you specified in your request. You can perform verification using either email or DNS. This topic discusses email validation. For information about DNS validation, see Use DNS to Validate Domain Ownership.

Note
Validation applies only to certificates provided by AWS Certificate Manager (ACM). ACM does not validate domain ownership for imported certificates. If you have trouble validating an ACM Certificate, see Troubleshoot Certificate Validation Problems. If you are not receiving email, see Not Receiving Validation Email.

AWS Certificate Manager (ACM) sends email to the 3 contact addresses listed in WHOIS and to 5 common system addresses for each domain that you specify. That is, up to 8 email messages will be sent for every domain name and subject alternative name that you include in your request. For example, if you specify only 1 domain name, you will receive up to 8 email messages. To validate, you must act on 1 of these 8 messages within 72 hours. If you specify 3 domain names, you will receive up to 24 messages. To validate, you must act on at least 3 of these emails, 1 for each name that you specified, within 72 hours.

Email is sent to the following three registered contact addresses in WHOIS:

- Domain registrant
- Technical contact
- Administrative contact

Note
Some registrars allow you to hide your contact information in your WHOIS listing, and others allow you to substitute your real email address with a privacy (or proxy) address. To prevent problems with receiving the domain validation email from ACM, ensure that your contact information is visible in WHOIS. If your WHOIS listing shows a privacy email address, ensure that email sent to that address is forwarded to your real email address. Or simply list your real email address instead.

If you use the console to request a certificate, ACM performs an MX lookup to determine which servers accept email for your domain and sends mail to the following five common system addresses for first domain found. If you use the RequestCertificate API or the request-certificate AWS CLI command, ACM does not perform an MX lookup. Instead, it sends email to the domain name you specify in the `DomainName` parameter or in the optional `ValidationDomain` parameter. For more information, see MX Record.

- administrator@*your_domain_name*
- hostmaster@*your_domain_name*
- postmaster@*your_domain_name*
- webmaster@*your_domain_name*
- admin@*your_domain_name*

For more information about how ACM determines the email addresses for your domains, see (Optional) Configure Email for Your Domain.

The console shows where the validation email messages have been sent for the first domain name you specify in your request. The email is sent from **no-reply@certificates.amazon.com**.

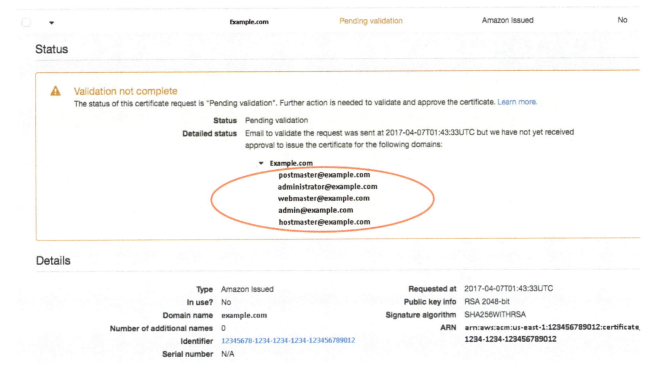

Note

There is an exception to the process described above. If you request an ACM Certificate for a domain name that begins with **www** or a wildcard asterisk (*), ACM removes the leading **www** or asterisk and sends email to the administrative addresses. These addresses are formed by prepending admin@, administrator@, hostmaster@, postmaster@, and webmaster@ to the remaining portion of the domain name. For example, if you request an ACM Certificate for www.example.com, email is sent to admin@example.com rather than to admin@www.example.com. Likewise, if you request an ACM Certificate for *.test.example.com, email is sent to admin@test.example.com. The remaining common administrative addresses are similarly formed.

Note

Ensure that email is sent to the administrative addresses for an apex domain, such as `example.com`, rather than to the administrative addresses for a subdomain, such as `test.example.com`. To do that, specify the `ValidationDomain` option in the RequestCertificate API or the request-certificate AWS CLI command. This feature is not currently supported when you use the console to request a certificate.

The following example shows the validation email that is sent for every domain name that you specify in your certificate request.

Greetings from Amazon Web Services,

We received a request to issue an SSL/TLS certificate for **www.example.com**.

Verify that the domain, AWS account ID, and certificate identifier below correspond to a request from you or someone in your organization.

Domain: **www.example.com**
AWS account number: **1234-5678-9012**
AWS Region name: **eu-central-1**
Certificate identifier: **12345678-90ab-cdef-1234-567890abcdef**

To approve this request, go to **Amazon Certificate Approvals**
(https://certificates.amazon.com/approvals?code=12345678-90ab-cdef-1234-567890abcdef&context=fedcba09-8765-4321-fedc-ba0987654321-1234567890abcdef12345678) and follow the instructions on the page.

If you choose not to approve this request, you do not need to do anything.

Choose the link that sends you to the Amazon Certificate Approvals website and then choose **I Approve**.

Amazon Web Services (AWS) has received a request to issue an SSL certificate for www.example.com. You are listed as one of the authorized representatives for this this domain name. Your authorization is required prior to issuing this certificate.

Verify that the domain name, AWS account ID, and certificate identifier below correspond to a request from you or a person authorized to request certificates for this domain name.

Domain name	www.example.com
AWS account number	1234-5678-9012
AWS Region	eu-central-1
Certificate identifier	12345678-90ab-cdef-1234-567890abcdef
	Review the information presented above and click **I Approve** only if you recognize the request and the account requesting it. By clicking **I Approve**, you authorize Amazon to request a certificate for the above domain name.

I Approve

If you choose not to approve this request, close this page.

If you have concerns about the validity of this request, forward the email you received with a brief explanation of your concern to:validation-questions@amazon.com

After choosing **I Approve**, a website opens to indicate that your request was successful.

Success!

You have approved an SSL/TLS certificate for the domain name www.example.com

Domain name	www.example.com
AWS account number	1234-5678-9012
AWS Region	eu-central-1
Arn	arn:aws:acm:eu-central-1:123456789012:certificate/12345678-90ab-cdef-1234-567890abcdef

Once all the domain names in the certificate request are approved, the authorized AWS account holder can review the certificate via the AWS Management Console, CLI, or API, or provision the certificate for use with integrated services, such as Amazon CloudFront or Elastic Load Balancing. For more information refer to the AWS Certificate Manager User Guide.

You can navigate back to the ACM console by clicking a link on the success page. It can take up to several hours for ACM to validate the domain name and issue the certificate. During this time, ACM shows the validation status as **Pending validation**. After validating the domain name, ACM changes the validation status to **Success**. After AWS issues the certificate, ACM changes the certificate status to **Issued**.

List ACM–Managed Certificates

You can use the ACM console or AWS CLI to list the certificates managed by ACM

Topics

- List Certificates (Console)
- List Certificates (CLI)

List Certificates (Console)

Display Certificate Information

Each certificates occupies a row in the console. By default, the following columns are displayed for each certificate:

- **Domain Name** – The fully qualified domain name for the certificate.
- **Additional Names** – Additional names that are supported by this certificate.
- **Status** – Certificate status. This can be any of the following values:
  - Pending validation
  - Issued
  - Inactive
  - Expired
  - Revoked
  - Failed
  - Timed out
- **In Use?** – Whether the ACM Certificate is actively associated with an AWS service such as Elastic Load Balancing or CloudFront. The value can be **No** or **Yes**.

Customize the Console Display

You can select the columns that you want to display by choosing the gear icon ( ) in the upper right corner of the console. You can select from among the following columns.

Show columns   ✕

Select which columns you would like to show/hide:

☑ Domain name
☑ Additional names
☐ Created at
☑ Status
☐ Signature algorithm
☐ Key algorithm
☐ Not before
☐ Not after
☐ Subject
☐ Issuer
☐ Revocation reason
☐ Serial
☐ Revoked at
☑ In use?
☐ Arn

List Certificates (CLI)

You can use the list-certificates command to list your ACM-managed certificates.

```
aws acm list-certificates --max-items 10
```

The `list-certificates` command outputs the following information.

```
{
    "CertificateSummaryList": [
        {
            "CertificateArn": "arn:aws:acm:region:account:certificate
                /123456789012-1234-1234-1234-12345678",
            "DomainName": "example.com"
        },
        {
            "CertificateArn": "arn:aws:acm:region:account:certificate
                /123456789012-1234-1234-1234-12345678",
            "DomainName": "mydomain.com"
        }
    ]
}
```

By default, only certificates that are supported by Services Integrated with AWS Certificate Manager are listed. That is, only certificates with **keyTypes** `RSA_1024` and `RSA_2048` are returned. To see other certificates that you own or control that use a different algorithm and bit size, use the `--includes` parameter as shown in the following example. The parameter allows you to specify a member of the Filters structure.

```
1 aws acm list-certificates --max-items 10 --includes keyTypes=RSA_4096
```

Describe ACM Certificates

You can use the ACM console or the AWS CLI to list metadata about your certificates.

Topics

- Describe Certificates (Console)
- Describe Certificates (CLI)

Describe Certificates (Console)

To show certificate metadata, select the arrow to the immediate left of the domain name. The console displays information similar to the following.

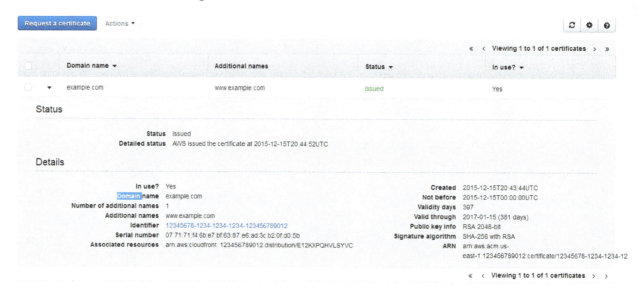

Describe Certificates (CLI)

You can use the AWS CLI to get information about an issued certificate, delete a certificate, or resend validation email.

Retrieve ACM Certificate Fields

You can use the describe-certificate command list the metadata for a certificate.

```
1 aws acm describe-certificate --certificate-arn arn:aws:acm:region:account:certificate
    /12345678-1234-1234-1234-123456789012
```

The `describe-certificate` command outputs the following information.

```
1 {
2     "Certificate": {
3         "CertificateArn": "arn:aws:acm:region:account:certificate
            /12345678-1234-1234-1234-123456789012",
4         "Status": "EXPIRED",
5         "Options": {
6             "CertificateTransparencyLoggingPreference": "ENABLED"
7         },
```

```
 8         "SubjectAlternativeNames": [
 9             "example.com",
10             "www.example.com"
11         ],
12         "DomainName": "gregpe.com",
13         "NotBefore": 1450137600.0,
14         "RenewalEligibility": "INELIGIBLE",
15         "NotAfter": 1484481600.0,
16         "KeyAlgorithm": "RSA-2048",
17         "InUseBy": [
18             "arn:aws:cloudfront::account:distribution/E12KXPQHVLSYVC"
19         ],
20         "SignatureAlgorithm": "SHA256WITHRSA",
21         "CreatedAt": 1450212224.0,
22         "IssuedAt": 1450212292.0,
23         "KeyUsages": [
24             {
25                 "Name": "DIGITAL_SIGNATURE"
26             },
27             {
28                 "Name": "KEY_ENCIPHERMENT"
29             }
30         ],
31         "Serial": "07:71:71:f4:6b:e7:bf:63:87:e6:ad:3c:b2:0f:d0:5b",
32         "Issuer": "Amazon",
33         "Type": "AMAZON_ISSUED",
34         "ExtendedKeyUsages": [
35             {
36                 "OID": "1.3.6.1.5.5.7.3.1",
37                 "Name": "TLS_WEB_SERVER_AUTHENTICATION"
38             },
39             {
40                 "OID": "1.3.6.1.5.5.7.3.2",
41                 "Name": "TLS_WEB_CLIENT_AUTHENTICATION"
42             }
43         ],
44         "DomainValidationOptions": [
45             {
46                 "ValidationEmails": [
47                     "hostmaster@example.com",
48                     "admin@example.com",
49                     "postmaster@example.com",
50                     "webmaster@example.com",
51                     "administrator@example.com"
52                 ],
53                 "ValidationDomain": "example.com",
54                 "DomainName": "example.com"
55             },
56             {
57                 "ValidationEmails": [
58                     "hostmaster@example.com",
59                     "admin@example.com",
60                     "postmaster@example.com",
61                     "webmaster@example.com",
```

```
62                "administrator@example.com"
63              ],
64              "ValidationDomain": "www.example.com",
65              "DomainName": "www.example.com"
66          }
67      ],
68      "Subject": "CN=example.com"
69    }
70 }
```

Delete ACM–Managed Certificates

You can use the ACM console or the AWS CLI to delete a certificate.

Topics

- Delete Certificates (Console)
- Delete Certificates (CLI)

Delete Certificates (Console)

In the list of certificates, select the check box for the ACM Certificate that you want to delete. For **Actions**, choose **Delete**.

Note
You cannot delete an ACM Certificate that is being used by another AWS service. To delete a certificate that is in use, you must first remove the certificate association.

Delete Certificates (CLI)

You can use the delete-certificate command list the metadata for a certificate.

```
1 aws acm delete-certificate --certificate-arn arn:aws:acm:region:123456789012:certificate
    /12345678-1234-1234-1234-123456789012
```

Install ACM Certificates

You cannot use ACM to directly install your ACM Certificate on your AWS based website or application. You must use one of the services integrated with ACM. For more information, see Services Integrated with AWS Certificate Manager.

Resend Validation Email (Optional)

You can use email to validate that you own or control a domain. Each email contains a validation token that you can use to approve a certificate request. However, because the validation email required for the approval process can be blocked by spam filters or lost in transit, the validation token automatically expires after 72 hours. If you do not receive the original email or the token has expired, you can request that the email be resent.

Topics

- Resend Email (Console)
- Resend Email (CLI)

Resend Email (Console)

Select the check box for the pending certificate, choose **Actions**, and then choose **Resend validation email**. If the 72-hour period has passed and the certificate status has changed to **Timed out**, you cannot resend validation email.

Note
The preceding information applies only to certificates provided by ACM and only to certificates that use email validation. Validation email is not required for certificates that you imported into ACM.

Note
Resending validation email applies only to certificates that use email validation, not DNS validation. For more information about DNS domain validation, see Use DNS to Validate Domain Ownership.

Resend Email (CLI)

You can use the resend-validation-email command to resend email.

```
1 aws acm resend-validation-email --certificate-arn arn:aws:acm:region:account:certificate
    /12345678-1234-1234-1234-123456789012 --validation-domain example.com
```

Note
The resend-validation-email command applies only to ACM certificates for which you are using email validation. Validation is not required for certificates that you have imported into ACM or for private certificates that you manage using ACM.

Managed Renewal for ACM's Amazon-Issued Certificates

ACM provides managed renewal for your Amazon-issued SSL/TLS certificates. This means that ACM tries to renew the certificates before they expire. If possible, ACM renews your certificates automatically with no action required from you.

Note
Automatic renewal is not available for either imported certificates or for certificates associated with Route 53 private hosted zones. You must renew these manually. For more information, see How Manual Domain Validation Works .

Note
When ACM renews a certificate, the certificate's Amazon Resource Name (ARN) remains the same. Also, ACM Certificates are regional resources. If you have certificates for the same domain name in multiple AWS Regions, ACM renews each of these certificates independently.

Important
Your ACM Certificate must be actively associated with a supported AWS service before it can be automatically renewed. For information about the resources that ACM supports, see Services Integrated with AWS Certificate Manager.

For more information about managed certificate renewal, see the following topics. If you encounter problems with managed renewal, see Troubleshoot Managed Certificate Renewal Problems.

Topics

- How Domain Validation Works
- Check a Certificate's Renewal Status
- Request a Domain Validation Email for Certificate Renewal

How Domain Validation Works

Before renewing a certificate, ACM tries to automatically validate each domain name in the certificate. For more information, see How Automatic Domain Validation Works. If ACM can't automatically validate a domain name, it notifies you that you need to take action to manually validate it. For more information, see When Automatic Validation Fails. If the certificate is in use (associated with an AWS service that is integrated with ACM) and if all of the domain names in the certificate can be validated, ACM renews the certificate.

Topics

- How Automatic Domain Validation Works
- When Automatic Validation Fails

How Automatic Domain Validation Works

To validate a domain, ACM sends automated, periodic HTTPS requests to it. For domains that start with `www.`, ACM also sends HTTPS requests to the parent domain. For example, if your domain is `www.example.com`, ACM sends periodic requests to `www.example.com` and to `example.com`. For domains that don't start with `www.`, ACM also sends HTTPS requests to `www.domain`. ACM treats wildcard domain names (for example, `*.example.com`) the same as the parent domain. For examples, see the following table.

Note
If any HTTPS connection attempt is successful, ACM attempts to renew the certificate automatically.

Example domain names that ACM uses for automatic validation

Domain name in the certificate	Domain names that ACM use for automatic validation
example.com	example.com www.example.com
www.example.com	www.example.com example.com
.example.com	example.com www.example.com
subdomain.example.com	subdomain.example.com www.subdomain.example.com
www.subdomain.example.com	www.subdomain.example.com subdomain.example.com
.subdomain.example.com	subdomain.example.com www.subdomain.example.com

If ACM successfully establishes an HTTPS connection, ACM examines the certificate that is returned to ensure it matches the one that ACM is renewing. If the certificate matches, ACM considers the domain name validated.

When Automatic Validation Fails

If ACM is unable to automatically validate one or more domain names in a certificate, ACM notifies you that you need to take action to manually validate the domain. A domain can require manual validation for the following reasons:

- ACM can't establish an HTTPS connection with the domain.
- The certificate that is returned in the response to the HTTPS requests doesn't match the one that ACM is renewing.

When your certificate is 45 days from expiration and one or more domain names in the certificate requires manual validation, ACM notifies you in the following ways:

By email to the domain owner (email validation)

If you originally used email validation when you requested the certificate, ACM sends email to the domain owner for each domain name that requires manual validation. To ensure that this email can be received, the domain owner must correctly configure email for each domain. For more information, see (Optional) Configure Email for Your Domain. The email contains a link that you can follow to perform the validation. This link expires after 72 hours. If necessary, you can use the AWS Certificate Manager console, AWS CLI, or API to request that ACM resend the domain validation email. For more information, see Request a Domain Validation Email for Certificate Renewal.

** By email to your AWS account (DNS validation)**

If you originally used DNS validation when you requested your certificate, ACM sends email to the address associated with your AWS account. The email informs you that ACM encountered a problem when attempting to renew your certificate. The most likely problems are that the original CNAME record is no longer in place or that your certificate is not associated with an AWS service that is integrated with ACM. If you want to validate your domain and renew your certificate, you must edit your DNS configuration to ensure that the original CNAME record is in place. In addition, and you must make sure that your ACM Certificate is in use. For more information about DNS validation, see Use DNS to Validate Domain Ownership.

By notification in your AWS Personal Health Dashboard

ACM sends notifications to your AWS Personal Health Dashboard to let you know that one or more domain names in the certificate require renewal. ACM sends these notifications when your certificate is 45 days, 30 days, 15 days, 7 days, 3 days, and 1 day from expiration. These notifications are informational only.

Check a Certificate's Renewal Status

You can use the AWS Certificate Manager console, the ACM API, the AWS CLI, or the Personal Health Dashboard to check the renewal status of an ACM Certificate. If you use the console, AWS CLI, or ACM API, certificate renewal can have one of the four possible status values listed below. Similar values are displayed if you use the Personal Health Dashboard.

Pending automatic renewal
ACM is attempting to automatically validate the domain names in the certificate. For more information, see How Domain Validation Works. No further action is required.

Pending validation
ACM couldn't automatically validate one or more domain names in the certificate. You must take action to validate these domain names or the certificate won't be renewed. If you originally used email validation for the certificate, look for an email from ACM and then follow the link in that email to perform the validation. If you used DNS validation, check to make sure your DNS record exists and that your certificate remains in use.

Success
All domain names in the certificate are validated, and ACM renewed the certificate. No further action is required.

Failed
One or more domain names were not validated before the certificate expired, and ACM did not renew the certificate. You can request a new certificate.

Note
It can take up to several hours for changes to the certificate status to become available.

Topics

- Check the status (console)
- Check the status (API)
- Check the status (CLI)
- Check the status (PHD)

Check the status (console)

The following procedure discusses how to use the ACM console to check the renewal status of an ACM Certificate.

1. Open the AWS Certificate Manager console at https://console.aws.amazon.com/acm/home.

2. Expand a certificate to view its details.

3. Find the **Renewal Status** in the **Details** section. If you don't see the status, ACM hasn't started the managed renewal process for this certificate.

Check the status (API)

For a Java example that shows how to use the DescribeCertificate action to check the status, see Describing a Certificate.

Check the status (CLI)

The following example shows how to check the status of your ACM certificate renewal with the AWS Command Line Interface (AWS CLI).

```
1 $ aws acm describe-certificate --certificate-arn arn:aws:acm:region:123456789012:certificate/97
    b4deb6-8983-4e39-918e-ef1378924e1e
```

In the response, note the value in the `RenewalStatus` field. If you don't see the `RenewalStatus` field, ACM hasn't started the managed renewal process for your certificate.

Check the status (PHD)

ACM attempts to automatically renew your ACM Certificate sixty days prior to expiration. See How Domain Validation Works. If ACM cannot automatically renew your certificate, it sends certificate renewal event notices to your Personal Health Dashboard at 45 day, 30 day, 15 day, 7 day, 3 day, and 1 day intervals from expiration to inform you that you need to take action. The Personal Health Dashboard is part of the AWS Health service. It requires no setup and can be viewed by any user that is authenticated in your account. For more information, see AWS Health User Guide.

To use the Personal Health Dashboard:

1. Log in to the Personal Health Dashboard at https://phd.aws.amazon.com/phd/home#/.

2. Choose **Event log**.

3. For **Filter by tags or attributes**, choose **Service**.

4. Choose **Certificate Manager**.

5. Choose **Apply**.

6. For **Event category** choose **Scheduled Change**.

7. Choose **Apply**.

If ACM has recently renewed an ACM Certificate, you will see information similar to the following.

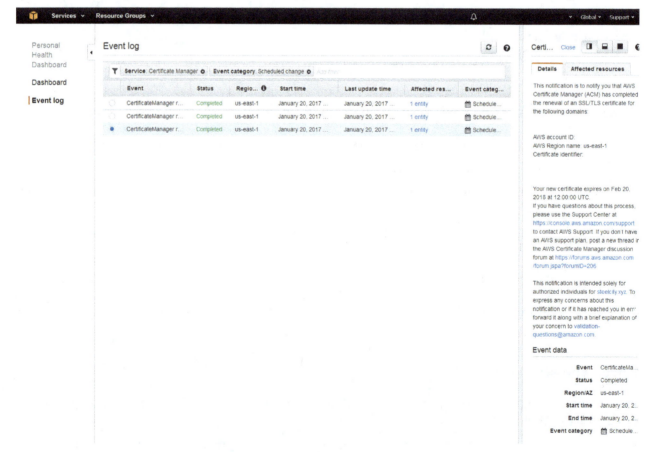

Request a Domain Validation Email for Certificate Renewal

After you have configured contact email addresses for your domain (see (Optional) Configure Email for Your Domain), you can use the AWS Certificate Manager console or the ACM API to request that ACM send you a domain validation email for your certificate renewal. You should do this in the following circumstances:

- You used email validation when initially requesting your ACM Certificate.
- Your certificate's renewal status is **pending validation**. For information about determining a certificate's renewal status, see Check a Certificate's Renewal Status.
- You didn't receive or can't find the original domain validation email that ACM sent for certificate renewal.

To request that ACM resend the domain validation email (console)

1. Open the AWS Certificate Manager console at https://console.aws.amazon.com/acm/home.

2. Select the check box next to the certificate that requires manual domain validation. Then choose **Actions, Resend validation email.**

To request that ACM resend the domain validation email (ACM API)
Use the ResendValidationEmail operation in the ACM API. In doing so, pass the ARN of the certificate, the domain that requires manual validation, and domain where you want to receive the domain validation emails. The following example shows how to do this with the AWS CLI. This example contains line breaks to make it easier to read.

```
1 $ aws acm resend-validation-email --certificate-arn arn:aws:acm:us-east-2:111122223333:
      certificate/97b4deb6-8983-4e39-918e-ef1378924e1e
2                                    --domain subdomain.example.com
3                                    --validation-domain example.com
```

Importing Certificates into AWS Certificate Manager

In addition to requesting SSL/TLS certificates provided by AWS Certificate Manager (ACM), you can import certificates that you obtained outside of AWS. You might do this because you already obtained a certificate from a third-party issuer, or because the certificates provided by ACM do not meet your requirements.

After you import an SSL/TLS certificate obtained outside of AWS and associated it with services integrated with ACM, you can reimport that certificate while preserving its associations.

After you import a certificate, you can use it with the AWS services that are integrated with ACM. The certificates that you import work the same as those provided by ACM, with one important exception: ACM does not provide managed renewal for imported certificates.

Important

You are responsible for monitoring the expiration date of your imported certificates and for renewing them before they expire. If you import a new certificate with the same ARN as the expiring certificate, the new certificate replaces the old one. In addition, ACM associates the new certificate with the same services and resources as the old certificate.

Important

We recommend that you do not pin an ACM Certificate. For more information, see Certificate Pinning and Troubleshoot Certificate Pinning Problems.

To renew an imported certificate, you can obtain a new certificate from your certificate issuer and then import it to ACM, or you can request a new certificate from ACM.

All certificates in ACM are regional resources, including the certificates that you import. To use the same certificate with Elastic Load Balancing load balancers in different AWS regions, you must import the certificate into each region where you want to use it. To use a certificate with Amazon CloudFront, you must import it into the US East (N. Virginia) region. For more information, see Supported Regions.

For information about how to import certificates into ACM, see the following topics. If you encounter problems importing a certificate, see Troubleshoot Certificate Importing Problems.

Topics

- Prerequisites for Importing Certificates
- Certificate and Key Format for Importing
- Import a Certificate
- Reimport a Certificate

Prerequisites for Importing Certificates

To import a self–signed SSL/TLS certificate into ACM, you must provide the certificate and its private key. To import a signed certificate, you must also include the certificate chain. Your certificate must satisfy the following criteria:

- The certificate must specify an algorithm and key size. Currently, the following public key algorithms are supported by ACM:
  - 1024-bit RSA (`RSA_1024`)
  - 2048-bit RSA (`RSA_2048`)
  - 4096-bit RSA (`RSA_4096`)
  - Elliptic Prime Curve 256 bit (`EC_prime256v1`)
  - Elliptic Prime Curve 384 bit (`EC_secp384r1`)
  - Elliptic Prime Curve 521 bit (`EC_secp521r1`)

Important
Note that integrated services allow only algorithms and key sizes they support to be associated with their resources. Further, their support differs depending on whether the certificate is imported into IAM or into ACM. For more information, see the documentation for each service.
For Elastic Load Balancing, see HTTPS Listeners for Your Application Load Balancer. For CloudFront, see Supported SSL/TLS Protocols and Ciphers.

- The certificate must be an SSL/TLS X.509 version 3 certificate. It must contain a public key, the fully qualified domain name (FQDN) for your website, and information about the issuer. The certificate can be self-signed by your private key or by the private key of an issuing CA. If your certificate is signed by a CA, you must include the certificate chain when you import your certificate.
- The certificate must be valid at the time of import. You cannot import a certificate before its validity period begins or after it expires. The `NotBefore` certificate field contains the validity start date, and the `NotAfter` field contains the end date.
- The private key must be unencrypted. You cannot import a private key that is protected by a password or passphrase.
- The certificate, private key, and certificate chain must be PEM–encoded. For more information and examples, see Certificate and Key Format for Importing.

Certificate and Key Format for Importing

The certificate, private key, and certificate chain must be PEM–encoded. PEM stands for Privacy Enhanced Mail. The PEM format is often used to represent certificates, certificate requests, certificate chains, and keys. The typical extension for a PEM–formatted file is `.pem`, but it doesn't need to be. The following examples illustrate the format. Note that if you edit any of the characters in a PEM file incorrectly or if you add one or more spaces to the end of any line, the certificate, certificate chain, or private key will be invalid.

Example PEM–encoded certificate

```
1 -----BEGIN CERTIFICATE------
2 Base64encoded certificate
3 -----END CERTIFICATE-----
```

Example PEM–encoded certificate chain

A certificate chain contains one or more certificates. You can use a text editor, the `copy` command in Windows, or the Linux `cat` command to concatenate your certificate files into a chain. The certificates must be concatenated in order so that each directly certifies the one preceding. Copy the root CA certificate last. The following example contains three certificates, but your certificate chain might contain more or fewer.

Do not copy your certificate into the certificate chain.

```
1 -----BEGIN CERTIFICATE------
2 Base64encoded certificate
3 -----END CERTIFICATE-----
4 -----BEGIN CERTIFICATE------
5 Base64encoded certificate
6 -----END CERTIFICATE-----
7 -----BEGIN CERTIFICATE------
8 Base64encoded certificate
9 -----END CERTIFICATE-----
```

Example PEM–encoded private keys

X.509 version 3 certificates utilize public key algorithms. When you create an X.509 certificate or certificate request, you specify the algorithm and the key bit size that must be used to create the private–public key pair. The public key is placed in the certificate or request. You must keep the associated private key secret. Specify the private key when you import the certificate. The key must be unencrypted. The following example shows an RSA private key.

```
1 -----BEGIN RSA PRIVATE KEY------
2 Base64encoded private key
3 -----END RSA PRIVATE KEY-----
```

The next example shows a PEM–encoded elliptic curve private key. Depending on how you create the key, the parameters block might not be included. If the parameters block is included, ACM removes it before using the key during the import process.

```
1 -----BEGIN EC PARAMETERS------
2 Base64encoded parameters
3 -----END EC PARAMETERS-----
4 -----BEGIN EC PRIVATE KEY------
5 Base64encoded private key
6 -----END EC PRIVATE KEY-----
```

Import a Certificate

The following example shows the CloudTrail log entry that records a call to the ACM ImportCertificate API operation.

```
1  {
2    "eventVersion": "1.04",
3    "userIdentity": {
4      "type": "IAMUser",
5      "principalId": "AIDACKCEVSQ6C2EXAMPLE",
6      "arn": "arn:aws:iam::111122223333:user/Alice",
7      "accountId": "111122223333",
8      "accessKeyId": "AKIAIOSFODNN7EXAMPLE",
9      "userName": "Alice"
10   },
11   "eventTime": "2016-10-04T16:01:30Z",
12   "eventSource": "acm.amazonaws.com",
13   "eventName": "ImportCertificate",
14   "awsRegion": "ap-southeast-2",
15   "sourceIPAddress": "54.240.193.129",
16   "userAgent": "Coral/Netty",
17   "requestParameters": {
18     "privateKey": {
19       "hb": [
20         byte,
21         byte,
22         byte,
23         ...
24       ],
25       "offset": 0,
26       "isReadOnly": false,
27       "bigEndian": true,
28       "nativeByteOrder": false,
29       "mark": -1,
30       "position": 0,
31       "limit": 1674,
32       "capacity": 1674,
33       "address": 0
34     },
35     "certificateChain": {
36       "hb": [
37         byte,
38         byte,
39         byte,
40         ...
41       ],
42       "offset": 0,
43       "isReadOnly": false,
44       "bigEndian": true,
45       "nativeByteOrder": false,
46       "mark": -1,
47       "position": 0,
48       "limit": 2105,
49       "capacity": 2105,
```

```
50        "address": 0
51      },
52      "certificate": {
53        "hb": [
54          byte,
55          byte,
56          byte,
57          ...
58        ],
59        "offset": 0,
60        "isReadOnly": false,
61        "bigEndian": true,
62        "nativeByteOrder": false,
63        "mark": -1,
64        "position": 0,
65        "limit": 2503,
66        "capacity": 2503,
67        "address": 0
68      }
69    },
70    "responseElements": {
71      "certificateArn": "arn:aws:acm:ap-southeast-2:111122223333:certificate/6ae06649-ea82-4b58-90
          ee-dc05870d7e99"
72    },
73    "requestID": "cf1f3db7-8a4b-11e6-88c8-196af94bb7be",
74    "eventID": "fb443118-bfaa-4c90-95c1-beef21e07f8e",
75    "eventType": "AwsApiCall",
76    "recipientAccountId": "111122223333"
77  }
```

Reimport a Certificate

If you imported a certificate and associated it with other AWS services, you can reimport that certificate before it expires while preserving the AWS service associations of the original certificate. For more information about AWS services integrated with ACM, see Services Integrated with AWS Certificate Manager.

The following conditions apply when you reimport a certificate:

- You can add or remove domain names.
- You cannot remove all of the domain names from a certificate.
- You can add new **Key Usage** extensions but existing extension values cannot be removed.
- You can add new **Extended Key Usage** extensions but existing extension values cannot be removed.
- The key type and size cannot be changed.

Topics

- Reimporting Using the Console
- Reimporting Using the AWS CLI

Reimporting Using the Console

The following example shows how to reimport a certificate using the AWS Management Console.

1. Open the ACM console at https://console.aws.amazon.com/acm/home.

2. Select or expand the certificate to reimport.

3. Open the details pane of the certificate and choose the **Reimport certificate** button. If you selected the certificate by checking the box beside its name, choose **Reimport certificate** on the **Actions** menu.

4. For **Certificate body**, paste the PEM-encoded end-entity certificate.

5. For **Certificate private key**, paste the unencrypted PEM-encoded private key associated with the certificate's public key. **Important**
Currently, Services Integrated with AWS Certificate Manager support only the `RSA_1024` and `RSA_2048` algorithms.

6. (Optional) For **Certificate chain**, paste the PEM-encoded certificate chain. The certificate chain includes the end-entity certificate, zero or more certificates for all intermediate issuing certification authorities, and the root certificate.

7. Choose **Review and import**.

8. Review the information about your certificate. If there are no errors, choose **Reimport**.

Reimporting Using the AWS CLI

The following example shows how to reimport a certificate using the AWS Command Line Interface (AWS CLI). The example assumes the following:

- The PEM-encoded certificate is stored in a file named `Certificate.pem`.
- The PEM-encoded certificate chain is stored in a file named `CertificateChain.pem`.
- The PEM-encoded, unencrypted private key is stored in a file named `PrivateKey.pem`.
- You have the ARN of the certificate you want to reimport.

To use the following example, replace the file names and the ARN with your own and type the command on one continuous line. The following example includes line breaks and extra spaces to make it easier to read.

Note
To reimport a certificate, you must specify the certificate ARN.

```
1    $ aws acm import-certificate --certificate file://Certificate.pem
2                                 --certificate-chain file://CertificateChain.pem
3                                 --private-key file://PrivateKey.pem
4                                 --certificate-arn arn:aws:acm:region:123456789012:certificate
                                  /12345678-1234-1234-1234-12345678901
```

If the `import-certificate` command is successful, it returns the Amazon Resource Name (ARN) of the certificate.

Tagging AWS Certificate Manager Certificates

A *tag* is a label that you can assign to an ACM Certificate. Each tag consists of a *key* and a *value*. You can use the AWS Certificate Manager console, AWS Command Line Interface (AWS CLI), or ACM API to add, view, or remove tags for ACM Certificates. You can choose which tags to display in the ACM console.

You can create custom tags that suit your needs. For example, you could tag multiple ACM Certificates with an `Environment = Prod` or `Environment = Beta` tag to identify which environment each ACM Certificate is intended for. The following list includes a few additional examples of other custom tags:

- `Admin = Alice`
- `Purpose = Website`
- `Protocol = TLS`
- `Registrar = Route53`

Other AWS resources also support tagging. You can, therefore, assign the same tag to different resources to indicate whether those resources are related. For example, you can assign a tag such as `Website = example.com` to the ACM Certificate, the load balancer, and other resources used for your example.com website.

Topics

- Tag Restrictions
- Managing Tags

Tag Restrictions

The following basic restrictions apply to ACM Certificate tags:

- The maximum number of tags per ACM Certificate is 50.
- The maximum length of a tag key is 127 characters.
- The maximum length of a tag value is 255 characters.
- Tag keys and values are case sensitive.
- The `aws:` prefix is reserved for AWS use; you cannot add, edit, or delete tags whose key begins with `aws:`. Tags that begin with `aws:` do not count against your tags-per-resource limit.
- If you plan to use your tagging schema across multiple services and resources, remember that other services may have other restrictions for allowed characters. Refer to the documentation for that service.
- ACM Certificate tags are not available for use in the AWS Management Console's Resource Groups and Tag Editor.

Managing Tags

You can add, edit, and delete tags by using the AWS Management Console, the AWS Command Line Interface, or the AWS Certificate Manager API.

Managing Tags (Console)

You can use the AWS Management Console to add, delete, or edit tags. You can also display tags in columns.

Adding a Tag (Console)

Use the following procedure to add tags by using the ACM console.

To add a tag to a certificate (console)

1. Sign into the AWS Management Console and open the AWS Certificate Manager console at https://console.aws.amazon.com/acm/home.

2. Choose the arrow next to the certificate that you want to tag.

3. In the details pane, scroll down to **Tags**.

4. Choose **Edit** and **Add Tag**.

5. Type a key and a value for the tag.

6. Choose **Save**.

Deleting a Tag (Console)

Use the following procedure to delete tags by using the ACM console.

To delete a tag (console)

1. Sign into the AWS Management Console and open the AWS Certificate Manager console at https://console.aws.amazon.com/acm/home.

2. Choose the arrow next to the certificate with a tag that you want to delete.

3. In the details pane, scroll down to **Tags**.

4. Choose **Edit**.

5. Choose the **X** next to the tag you want to delete.

6. Choose **Save**.

Editing a Tag (Console)

Use the following procedure to edit tags by using the ACM console.

To edit a tag (console)

1. Sign into the AWS Management Console and open the AWS Certificate Manager console at https://console.aws.amazon.com/acm/home.

2. Choose the arrow next to certificate you want to edit.

3. In the details pane, scroll down to **Tags**.

4. Choose **Edit**.

5. Modify the key or value of the tag you want to change.

6. Choose **Save**.

Showing Tags in Columns (Console)

Use the following procedure to show tags in columns in the ACM console.

To display tags in columns (console)

1. Sign into the AWS Management Console and open the AWS Certificate Manager console at https://console.aws.amazon.com/acm/home.

2. Choose the tags that you want to display as columns by choosing the gear icon in the upper right corner of the console.

3. Select the check box beside the tag that you want to display in a column.

Managing Tags (AWS Command Line Interface)

Refer to the following topics to learn how to add, list, and delete tags by using the AWS CLI.

- add-tags-to-certificate
- list-tags-for-certificate
- remove-tags-from-certificate

Managing Tags (AWS Certificate Manager API)

Refer to the following topics to learn how to add, list, and delete tags by using the API.

- AddTagsToCertificate
- ListTagsForCertificate
- RemoveTagsFromCertificate

Authentication and Access Control

Access to ACM requires credentials that AWS can use to authenticate your requests. The credentials must have permissions to access AWS resources such as ACM Certificates. The following sections provide details on how you can use AWS Identity and Access Management (IAM) and ACM to help secure your resources by controlling who can access them.

Topics

- Authentication
- Access Control

Authentication

You can access AWS as any of the following types of identities:

- **AWS account root user** – When you first create an AWS account, you begin with a single sign-in identity that has complete access to all AWS services and resources in the account. This identity is called the AWS account *root user* and is accessed by signing in with the email address and password that you used to create the account. We strongly recommend that you do not use the root user for your everyday tasks, even the administrative ones. Instead, adhere to the best practice of using the root user only to create your first IAM user. Then securely lock away the root user credentials and use them to perform only a few account and service management tasks.

- **IAM user** – An IAM user is an identity within your AWS account that has specific custom permissions (for example, permissions to create a directory in ACM). You can use an IAM user name and password to sign in to secure AWS webpages like the AWS Management Console, AWS Discussion Forums, or the AWS Support Center.

  In addition to a user name and password, you can also generate access keys for each user. You can use these keys when you access AWS services programmatically, either through one of the several SDKs or by using the AWS Command Line Interface (CLI). The SDK and CLI tools use the access keys to cryptographically sign your request. If you don't use AWS tools, you must sign the request yourself. ACM supports *Signature Version 4*, a protocol for authenticating inbound API requests. For more information about authenticating requests, see Signature Version 4 Signing Process in the *AWS General Reference*.

- **IAM role** – An IAM role is an IAM identity that you can create in your account that has specific permissions. It is similar to an *IAM user*, but it is not associated with a specific person. An IAM role enables you to obtain temporary access keys that can be used to access AWS services and resources. IAM roles with temporary credentials are useful in the following situations:

  - **Federated user access** – Instead of creating an IAM user, you can use existing user identities from AWS Directory Service, your enterprise user directory, or a web identity provider. These are known as *federated users*. AWS assigns a role to a federated user when access is requested through an identity provider. For more information about federated users, see Federated Users and Roles in the *IAM User Guide*.

  - **AWS service access** – You can use an IAM role in your account to grant an AWS service permissions to access your account's resources. For example, you can create a role that allows Amazon Redshift to access an Amazon S3 bucket on your behalf and then load data from that bucket into an Amazon

Redshift cluster. For more information, see Creating a Role to Delegate Permissions to an AWS Service in the *IAM User Guide*.

- **Applications running on Amazon EC2** – You can use an IAM role to manage temporary credentials for applications that are running on an EC2 instance and making AWS API requests. This is preferable to storing access keys within the EC2 instance. To assign an AWS role to an EC2 instance and make it available to all of its applications, you create an instance profile that is attached to the instance. An instance profile contains the role and enables programs that are running on the EC2 instance to get temporary credentials. For more information, see Using an IAM Role to Grant Permissions to Applications Running on Amazon EC2 Instances in the *IAM User Guide*.

Access Control

You can have valid credentials to authenticate your requests, but unless you have permissions you cannot create or access ACM resources. For example, you must have permission to create, import, retrieve, or list certificates.

The following topics describe how to manage permissions. We recommend that you read the overview first.

- Overview of Managing Access to Your ACM Resources
- AWS–Managed Policies
- Customer Managed Policies
- Inline Policies
- ACM API Permissions: Actions and Resources Reference

Overview of Managing Access to Your ACM Resources

Every AWS resource belongs to an AWS account, and permissions to create or access the resources are defined in permissions policies in that account. An account administrator can attach permissions policies to IAM identities (that is, users, groups, and roles). Some services (including ACM) also support attaching permissions policies to resources.

Note

An *account administrator* (or administrator user) is a user with administrator permissions. For more information, see Creating an Admin User and Group in the *IAM User Guide*.

When managing permissions, you decide who gets the permissions, the resources they get permissions for, and the specific actions allowed.

Topics

- ACM Resources and Operations
- Understanding Resource Ownership
- Managing Access to ACM Certificates

ACM Resources and Operations

In ACM, the primary resource is a *certificate*. Certificates have unique Amazon Resource Names (ARNs) associated with them as shown in the following list.

- **ACM Certificate**

  ARN format:

  `arn:aws:acm:AWS region:AWS account ID:certificate/Certificate ID`

  Example ARN:

  `arn:aws:acm:us-west-2:123456789012:certificate/12345678-12ab-34cd-56ef-12345678`

Understanding Resource Ownership

A *resource owner* is the AWS account that created a resource. That is, the resource owner is the AWS account of the *principal entity* that authenticates the request that created the resource. (A principle entity can be an AWS account root user, an IAM user, or an IAM role.) The following examples illustrate how this works.

- If you use the credentials of your AWS account root user to create an ACM Certificate, your AWS account owns the certificate.
- If you create an IAM user in your AWS account, you can grant that user permission to create an ACM Certificate. However, the account to which that user belongs owns the certificate.
- If you create an IAM role in your AWS account and grant it permission to create an ACM Certificate, anyone who can assume the role can create a certificate. However, the account to which the role belongs owns the certificate.

Managing Access to ACM Certificates

A *permissions policy* describes who has access to what. This section explains the available options for creating permissions policies.

Note

This section discusses using IAM in the context of ACM. It doesn't provide detailed information about the IAM service. For complete IAM documentation, see the IAM User Guide. For information about IAM policy syntax and descriptions, see AWS IAM Policy Reference.

You can use IAM to create policies that apply permissions to IAM users, groups, and roles. These are called *identity–based policies*. IAM offers the following types of identity–based policies:

- **AWS–managed policies** – Policies that are created and managed by AWS. These are standalone policies that you can attach to multiple users, groups, and roles in your AWS account.
- **Customer–managed policies** – Policies that you create and manage in your AWS account and which you can attach to multiple users, groups, and roles. You have more precise control when using customer managed policies than you have when using AWS managed policies.
- **Inline policies** – Policies that you create and manage and which you embed directly into a single user, group, or role.

Other services, such as Amazon S3, also support resource–based permissions policies. For example, you can attach a policy to an Amazon S3 bucket to manage access permissions to that bucket. ACM does not support resource-based policies.

AWS–Managed Policies

AWS managed policies are standalone identity–based policies that you can attach to multiple users, groups, and roles in your AWS account. AWS managed policies are created and managed by AWS. The following AWS managed policies are available for ACM. For more information about attaching managed policies to a user, group, or role, see Working with Managed Policies in the IAM User Guide.

To use an AWS managed policy, a user with administrative privileges must attach the policy to a user, role, or group. For more information about attaching AWS managed policies, see Attaching Managed Policies in the IAM User Guide.

Topics

- AWSCertificateManagerReadOnly
- AWSCertificateManagerFullAccess

AWSCertificateManagerReadOnly

This policy provides read–only access to ACM Certificates; it allows users to describe, list, and retrieve ACM Certificates.

```
1  {
2    "Version": "2012-10-17",
3    "Statement": {
4      "Effect": "Allow",
5      "Action": [
6        "acm:DescribeCertificate",
7        "acm:ListCertificates",
8        "acm:GetCertificate",
9        "acm:ListTagsForCertificate"
10     ],
11     "Resource": "*"
12   }
13 }
```

To view this AWS managed policy in the console, go to https://console.aws.amazon.com/iam/home#policies/arn: aws:iam::aws:policy/AWSCertificateManagerReadOnly.

AWSCertificateManagerFullAccess

This policy provides full access to all ACM actions and resources.

```
1  {
2    "Version": "2012-10-17",
3    "Statement": [{
4      "Effect": "Allow",
5      "Action": ["acm:*"],
6      "Resource": "*"
7    }]
8  }
```

To view this AWS managed policy in the console, go to https://console.aws.amazon.com/iam/home#policies/arn: aws:iam::aws:policy/AWSCertificateManagerFullAccess.

Customer Managed Policies

Customer managed policies are standalone identity–based policies that you create and which you can attach to multiple users, groups, or roles in your AWS account. You can manage and create policies using the AWS Management Console, the AWS Command Line Interface (AWS CLI), or the IAM API. For more information about using the console to administer customer managed policies, see the following topics in the IAM User Guide.

- Attaching Managed Policies
- Detaching Managed Policies
- Creating Customer Managed Policies
- Editing Customer Managed Policies
- Setting the Default Version of Customer Managed Policies
- Deleting Versions of Customer Managed Policies
- Deleting Customer Managed Policies

For more information about using the API, see Working with Managed Policies Using the AWS CLI or the IAM API

Inline Policies

Inline policies are policies that you create and manage and embed directly into a single user, group, or role. The following policy examples show how to assign permissions to perform ACM actions. For more information about attaching inline policies, see Working with Inline Policies in the IAM User Guide. You can use the AWS Management Console, the AWS Command Line Interface (AWS CLI), or the IAM API to create and embed inline policies.

Topics

- Listing Certificates
- Retrieving a Certificate
- Importing a Certificate
- Deleting a Certificate
- Read-Only Access to ACM
- Full Access to ACM
- Administrator Access to All AWS Resources

Listing Certificates

The following policy allows a user to list all of the ACM Certificates in the user's account.

```
1 {
2   "Version": "2012-10-17",
3   "Statement": [{
4     "Effect": "Allow",
5     "Action": "acm:ListCertificates",
6     "Resource": "*"
7   }]
8 }
```

Note
This permission is required for ACM Certificates to appear in the Elastic Load Balancing and CloudFront consoles.

Retrieving a Certificate

The following policy allows a user to retrieve a specific ACM Certificate.

```
1 {
2   "Version": "2012-10-17",
3   "Statement": {
4     "Effect": "Allow",
5     "Action": "acm:GetCertificate",
6     "Resource": "arn:aws:acm:us-east-1:123456789012:certificate
          /12345678-1234-1234-1234-123456789012"
7   }
8 }
```

Importing a Certificate

The following policy allows a user to import a certificate.

```
1 {
2   "Version": "2012-10-17",
3   "Statement": {
4     "Effect": "Allow",
5     "Action": "acm:ImportCertificate",
6     "Resource": "arn:aws:acm:ap-northeast-1:123456789012:certificate
        /12345678-1234-1234-1234-123456789012"
7   }
8 }
```

Deleting a Certificate

The following policy allows a user to delete a specific ACM Certificate.

```
1 {
2   "Version": "2012-10-17",
3   "Statement": {
4     "Effect": "Allow",
5     "Action": "acm:DeleteCertificate",
6     "Resource": "arn:aws:acm:us-east-1:123456789012:certificate
        /12345678-1234-1234-1234-123456789012"
7   }
8 }
```

Read-Only Access to ACM

The following policy allows a user to describe and list an ACM Certificate and to retrieve the ACM Certificate and certificate chain.

```
1  {
2    "Version": "2012-10-17",
3    "Statement": {
4      "Effect": "Allow",
5      "Action": [
6        "acm:DescribeCertificate",
7        "acm:ListCertificates",
8        "acm:GetCertificate",
9        "acm:ListTagsForCertificate"
10     ],
11     "Resource": "*"
12   }
13 }
```

Note
This policy is available as an AWS–managed policy in the AWS Management Console. For more information, see AWSCertificateManagerReadOnly. To view the managed policy in the console, go to https://console.aws. amazon.com/iam/home#policies/arn:aws:iam::aws:policy/AWSCertificateManagerReadOnly.

Full Access to ACM

The following policy allows a user to perform any ACM action.

```
1 {
2   "Version": "2012-10-17",
3   "Statement": [{
4     "Effect": "Allow",
5     "Action": ["acm:*"],
6     "Resource": "*"
7   }]
8 }
```

Note

This policy is available as an AWS–managed policy in the AWS Management Console. For more information, see AWSCertificateManagerFullAccess. To view the managed policy in the console, go to https://console.aws.amazon.com/iam/home#policies/arn:aws:iam::aws:policy/AWSCertificateManagerFullAccess.

Administrator Access to All AWS Resources

The following policy allows a user to perform any action on any AWS resource.

```
1 {
2   "Version": "2012-10-17",
3   "Statement": [{
4     "Effect": "Allow",
5     "Action": "*",
6     "Resource": "*"
7   }]
8 }
```

Note

This policy is available as an AWS–managed policy in the AWS Management Console. To view the managed policy in the console, go to https://console.aws.amazon.com/iam/home#policies/arn:aws:iam::aws:policy/AdministratorAccess.

ACM API Permissions: Actions and Resources Reference

When you are setting up access control and writing permissions policies that you can attach to an IAM identity (identity-based policies), you can use the following table as a reference. The first column in the table lists each ACM API operation. You specify actions in a policy's `Action` element. The remaining columns provide the additional information:

You can use the IAM policy elements in your ACM policies to express conditions. For a complete list, see Available Keys in the *IAM User Guide*.

Note
To specify an action, use the `acm:` prefix followed by the API operation name (for example, `acm: RequestCertificate`).

If you see an expand arrow () in the upper-right corner of the table, you can open the table in a new window. To close the window, choose the close button (**X**) in the lower-right corner.

ACM API Operations and Permissions

ACM API Operations	Required Permissions (API Actions)	Resources
AddTagsToCertificate	`acm:AddTagsToCertificate`	`arn:aws:acm:AWS_region :AWS_account_ID :certificate/ certificate_ID`
DeleteCertificate	`acm:DeleteCertificate`	`arn:aws:acm:AWS_region :AWS_account_ID :certificate/ certificate_ID`
DescribeCertificate	`acm:DescribeCertificate`	`arn:aws:acm:AWS_region :AWS_account_ID :certificate/ certificate_ID`
GetCertificate	`acm:GetCertificate`	`arn:aws:acm:AWS_region :AWS_account_ID :certificate/ certificate_ID`
ImportCertificate	`acm:ImportCertificate`	`arn:aws:acm:AWS_region :AWS_account_ID :certificate/ certificate_ID`
ListCertificates	`acm:ListCertificates`	`arn:aws:acm:AWS_region :AWS_account_ID :certificate/ certificate_ID`
ListTagsForCertificate	`acm: ListTagsForCertificate`	`arn:aws:acm:AWS_region :AWS_account_ID :certificate/ certificate_ID`
RemoveTagsFromCertificate	`acm: RemoveTagsFromCertificate`	`arn:aws:acm:AWS_region :AWS_account_ID :certificate/ certificate_ID`

ACM API Operations	Required Permissions (API Actions)	Resources
RequestCertificate	`acm:RequestCertificate`	`arn:aws:acm:AWS_region :AWS_account_ID :certificate/ certificate_ID`
ResendValidationEmail	`acm: ResendValidationEmail`	`arn:aws:acm:AWS_region :AWS_account_ID :certificate/ certificate_ID`

Using AWS CloudTrail

You can use CloudTrail to record API calls that are made by AWS Certificate Manager and by services integrated with ACM as discussed in the following topics.

Topics

- Logging AWS Certificate Manager API Calls with AWS CloudTrail
- Logging ACM-Related API Calls

Logging AWS Certificate Manager API Calls with AWS CloudTrail

AWS Certificate Manager (ACM) is integrated with AWS CloudTrail, a service that captures API calls, delivers the log files to an Amazon Simple Storage Service (Amazon S3) bucket that you specify, and maintains API call history. CloudTrail captures API calls from the AWS Certificate Manager console, CLI, or from your code. Using the information collected by CloudTrail, you can determine the request that was made to ACM, the IP address from which the request was made, who made the request, when it was made, and so on.

To learn more about CloudTrail, including how to configure and enable it, see the AWS CloudTrail User Guide.

When you enable CloudTrail logging in your AWS account, API calls made to ACM actions are tracked in CloudTrail log files. The ACM records are written with other AWS service records. CloudTrail determines when to create and write to a new log file based on a time period and file size.

The following ACM actions are supported:

- AddTagsToCertificate
- DeleteCertificate
- DescribeCertificate
- GetCertificate
- ImportCertificate
- ListCertificates
- ListTagsForCertificate
- RemoveTagsFromCertificate
- RequestCertificate
- ResendValidationEmail

Every log entry contains information about who generated the request. The user identity information in the log entry helps you determine whether the request was made with root or with IAM user credentials, with temporary security credentials for a role or federated user, or by another AWS service. For more information, see the CloudTrail userIdentity Element.

You can store your log files in your bucket for as long as you want, but you can also define Amazon S3 lifecycle rules to archive or delete log files automatically. By default, your log files are encrypted using Amazon S3 server-side encryption (SSE).

You can choose to have CloudTrail publish Amazon SNS notifications when new log files are delivered if you want to take quick action upon log delivery. For more information, see Configuring Amazon SNS Notifications for CloudTrail in the *AWS CloudTrail User Guide.*

You can also aggregate AWS Certificate Manager log files from multiple AWS regions and multiple AWS accounts into a single Amazon S3 bucket. For more information, see Receiving CloudTrail Log Files from Multiple Regions and Receiving CloudTrail Log Files from Multiple Accounts.

CloudTrail log files contain one or more log entries where each entry lists multiple JSON-formatted events. A log entry represents a single request from any source and includes information about the requested action, the date and time of the action, request parameters and so on. The log entries are not guaranteed to be in any particular order. That is, they are not an ordered trace of the public API calls. For more information about the fields that make up a log entry, see the CloudTrail Event Reference.

For examples of possible ACM CloudTrail entries, see the following topics.

Topics

- Adding Tags to a Certificate
- Deleting a Certificate
- Describing a Certificate
- Retrieving a Certificate
- Import a Certificate
- Listing Certificates

- Listing Tags for a Certificate
- Removing Tags from a Certificate
- Requesting a Certificate
- Resending Validation Email

Adding Tags to a Certificate

The following example shows how to use the AddTagsToCertificate function.

```
1 package com.amazonaws.samples;
2
3 import com.amazonaws.services.certificatemanager.AWSCertificateManagerClientBuilder;
4 import com.amazonaws.services.certificatemanager.AWSCertificateManager;
5 import com.amazonaws.services.certificatemanager.model.AddTagsToCertificateRequest;
6 import com.amazonaws.services.certificatemanager.model.AddTagsToCertificateResult;
7 import com.amazonaws.services.certificatemanager.model.Tag;
8
9 import com.amazonaws.services.certificatemanager.model.InvalidArnException;
10 import com.amazonaws.services.certificatemanager.model.InvalidTagException;
11 import com.amazonaws.services.certificatemanager.model.ResourceNotFoundException;
12 import com.amazonaws.services.certificatemanager.model.TooManyTagsException;
13
14 import com.amazonaws.AmazonClientException;
15
16 import com.amazonaws.auth.AWSCredentials;
17 import com.amazonaws.auth.profile.ProfileCredentialsProvider;
18 import com.amazonaws.auth.AWSStaticCredentialsProvider;
19 import com.amazonaws.regions.Regions;
20
21 import java.util.ArrayList;
22
23 /**
24  * This sample demonstrates how to use the AddTagsToCertificate function in the AWS Certificate
25  * Manager service.
26  *
27  * Input parameters:
28  *    CertificateArn - The ARN of the certificate to which to add one or more tags.
29  *    Tags - An array of Tag objects to add.
30  *
31  */
32
33 public class AWSCertificateManagerExample {
34
35     public static void main(String[] args) throws Exception {
36
37         // Retrieve your credentials from the C:\Users\name\.aws\credentials file in Windows
38         // or the ~/.aws/credentials file in Linux.
39         AWSCredentials credentials = null;
40         try {
41             credentials = new ProfileCredentialsProvider().getCredentials();
42         }
43         catch (Exception ex) {
44             throw new AmazonClientException("Cannot load your credentials from file.", ex);
45         }
46
47         // Create a client.
48         AWSCertificateManager client = AWSCertificateManagerClientBuilder.standard()
49                 .withRegion(Regions.US_EAST_1)
50                 .withCredentials(new AWSStaticCredentialsProvider(credentials))
```

```java
51                .build();
52
53      // Create tags.
54      Tag tag1 = new Tag();
55      tag1.setKey("Short_Name");
56      tag1.setValue("My_Cert");
57
58      Tag tag2 = new Tag()
59              .withKey("Purpose")
60              .withValue("Test");
61
62      // Add the tags to a collection.
63      ArrayList<Tag> tags = new ArrayList<Tag>();
64      tags.add(tag1);
65      tags.add(tag2);
66
67      // Create a request object and specify the ARN of the certificate.
68      AddTagsToCertificateRequest req = new AddTagsToCertificateRequest();
69      req.setCertificateArn("arn:aws:acm:region:account:certificate
              /12345678-1234-1234-1234-123456789012");
70      req.setTags(tags);
71
72      // Add tags to the specified certificate.
73      AddTagsToCertificateResult result = null;
74      try {
75          result = client.addTagsToCertificate(req);
76      }
77      catch(InvalidArnException ex)
78      {
79          throw ex;
80      }
81      catch(InvalidTagException ex)
82      {
83          throw ex;
84      }
85      catch(ResourceNotFoundException ex)
86      {
87          throw ex;
88      }
89      catch(TooManyTagsException ex)
90      {
91          throw ex;
92      }
93
94      // Display the result.
95      System.out.println(result);
96   }
97 }
```

Deleting a Certificate

The following example shows how to use the DeleteCertificate function. If succesful, the function returns an empty set {}.

```
 1 package com.amazonaws.samples;
 2
 3 import com.amazonaws.services.certificatemanager.AWSCertificateManagerClientBuilder;
 4 import com.amazonaws.services.certificatemanager.AWSCertificateManager;
 5 import com.amazonaws.services.certificatemanager.model.DeleteCertificateRequest;
 6 import com.amazonaws.services.certificatemanager.model.DeleteCertificateResult;
 7
 8 import com.amazonaws.auth.profile.ProfileCredentialsProvider;
 9 import com.amazonaws.auth.AWSStaticCredentialsProvider;
10 import com.amazonaws.auth.AWSCredentials;
11 import com.amazonaws.regions.Regions;
12
13 import com.amazonaws.services.certificatemanager.model.InvalidArnException;
14 import com.amazonaws.services.certificatemanager.model.ResourceInUseException;
15 import com.amazonaws.services.certificatemanager.model.ResourceNotFoundException;
16 import com.amazonaws.AmazonClientException;
17
18 /**
19  * This sample demonstrates how to use the DeleteCertificate function in the AWS Certificate
20  * Manager service.
21  *
22  * Input parameter:
23  *    CertificateArn - The ARN of the certificate to delete.
24  *
25  */
26
27 public class AWSCertificateManagerExample {
28
29     public static void main(String[] args) throws Exception{
30
31         // Retrieve your credentials from the C:\Users\name\.aws\credentials file in Windows
32         // or the ~/.aws/credentials file in Linux.
33         AWSCredentials credentials = null;
34         try {
35             credentials = new ProfileCredentialsProvider().getCredentials();
36         }
37         catch (Exception ex) {
38             throw new AmazonClientException("Cannot load the credentials from file.", ex);
39         }
40
41         // Create a client.
42         AWSCertificateManager client = AWSCertificateManagerClientBuilder.standard()
43                 .withRegion(Regions.US_EAST_1)
44                 .withCredentials(new AWSStaticCredentialsProvider(credentials))
45                 .build();
46
47         // Create a request object and specify the ARN of the certificate to delete.
48         DeleteCertificateRequest req = new DeleteCertificateRequest();
```

```
49      req.setCertificateArn("arn:aws:acm:region:account:certificate
            /12345678-1234-1234-1234-123456789012");
50
51      // Delete the specified certificate.
52      DeleteCertificateResult result = null;
53      try {
54          result = client.deleteCertificate(req);
55      }
56      catch (InvalidArnException ex)
57      {
58          throw ex;
59      }
60      catch (ResourceInUseException ex)
61      {
62          throw ex;
63      }
64      catch (ResourceNotFoundException ex)
65      {
66          throw ex;
67      }
68
69      // Display the result.
70      System.out.println(result);
71
72  }
73 }
```

Describing a Certificate

The following example shows how to use the DescribeCertificate function.

```
1  package com.amazonaws.samples;
2
3
4  import com.amazonaws.services.certificatemanager.AWSCertificateManagerClientBuilder;
5  import com.amazonaws.services.certificatemanager.AWSCertificateManager;
6  import com.amazonaws.services.certificatemanager.model.DescribeCertificateRequest;
7  import com.amazonaws.services.certificatemanager.model.DescribeCertificateResult;
8
9  import com.amazonaws.auth.profile.ProfileCredentialsProvider;
10 import com.amazonaws.auth.AWSStaticCredentialsProvider;
11 import com.amazonaws.auth.AWSCredentials;
12 import com.amazonaws.regions.Regions;
13
14 import com.amazonaws.services.certificatemanager.model.InvalidArnException;
15 import com.amazonaws.services.certificatemanager.model.ResourceNotFoundException;
16 import com.amazonaws.AmazonClientException;
17
18 /**
19  * This sample demonstrates how to use the DescribeCertificate function in the AWS Certificate
20  * Manager service.
21  *
22  * Input parameter:
23  *    CertificateArn - The ARN of the certificate to be described.
24  *
25  * Output parameter:
26  *    Certificate information
27  *
28  */
29
30 public class AWSCertificateManagerExample {
31
32     public static void main(String[] args) throws Exception{
33
34         // Retrieve your credentials from the C:\Users\name\.aws\credentials file in Windows
35         // or the ~/.aws/credentials file in Linux.
36         AWSCredentials credentials = null;
37         try {
38             credentials = new ProfileCredentialsProvider().getCredentials();
39         }
40         catch (Exception ex) {
41             throw new AmazonClientException("Cannot load the credentials from file.", ex);
42         }
43
44         // Create a client.
45         AWSCertificateManager client = AWSCertificateManagerClientBuilder.standard()
46                 .withRegion(Regions.US_EAST_1)
47                 .withCredentials(new AWSStaticCredentialsProvider(credentials))
48                 .build();
49
50         // Create a request object and set the ARN of the certificate to be described.
```

```
51    DescribeCertificateRequest req = new DescribeCertificateRequest();
52    req.setCertificateArn("arn:aws:acm:region:account:certificate
         /12345678-1234-1234-1234-123456789012");
53
54    DescribeCertificateResult result = null;
55    try{
56       result = client.describeCertificate(req);
57    }
58    catch (InvalidArnException ex)
59    {
60       throw ex;
61    }
62    catch (ResourceNotFoundException ex)
63    {
64       throw ex;
65    }
66
67    // Display the certificate information.
68    System.out.println(result);
69
70  }
71 }
```

If successful, the preceding example displays information similar to the following.

```
1 {
2     Certificate: {
3         CertificateArn: arn:aws:acm:region:account:certificate
               /12345678-1234-1234-1234-123456789012,
4         DomainName: www.example.com,
5         SubjectAlternativeNames: [www.example.com],
6         DomainValidationOptions: [{
7             DomainName: www.example.com,
8         }],
9         Serial: 10: 0a,
10        Subject: C=US,
11        ST=WA,
12        L=Seattle,
13        O=ExampleCompany,
14        OU=sales,
15        CN=www.example.com,
16        Issuer: ExampleCompany,
17        ImportedAt: FriOct0608: 17: 39PDT2017,
18        Status: ISSUED,
19        NotBefore: ThuOct0510: 14: 32PDT2017,
20        NotAfter: SunOct0310: 14: 32PDT2027,
21        KeyAlgorithm: RSA-2048,
22        SignatureAlgorithm: SHA256WITHRSA,
23        InUseBy: [],
24        Type: IMPORTED,
25    }
26 }
```

Retrieving a Certificate

The following CloudTrail example shows the results of a call to the GetCertificate API.

```
1  {
2      "Records": [{
3          "eventVersion": "1.04",
4          "userIdentity": {
5              "type": "IAMUser",
6              "principalId": "AIDACKCEVSQ6C2EXAMPLE",
7              "arn": "arn:aws:iam::123456789012:user/Alice",
8              "accountId": "123456789012",
9              "accessKeyId": "AKIAIOSFODNN7EXAMPLE",
10             "userName": "Alice"
11         },
12         "eventTime": "2016-03-18T00:00:41Z",
13         "eventSource": "acm.amazonaws.com",
14         "eventName": "GetCertificate",
15         "awsRegion": "us-east-1",
16         "sourceIPAddress": "192.0.2.0",
17         "userAgent": "aws-cli/1.9.15",
18         "requestParameters": {
19             "certificateArn": "arn:aws:acm:us-east-1:123456789012:certificate
                   /12345678-1234-1234-1234-123456789012"
20         },
21         "responseElements": {
22             "certificateChain":
23             "-----BEGIN CERTIFICATE-----
24             Base64-encoded certificate chain
25             -----END CERTIFICATE-----",
26             "certificate":
27             "-----BEGIN CERTIFICATE-----
28             Base64-encoded certificate
29             -----END CERTIFICATE-----"
30         },
31         "requestID": "744dd891-ec9c-11e5-ac34-d1e4dfe1a11b",
32         "eventID": "7aa4f909-00dd-478a-9a00-b2709bcad2bb",
33         "eventType": "AwsApiCall",
34         "recipientAccountId": "123456789012"
35     }]
36 }
```

Listing Certificates

The following example shows how to use the ListCertificates function.

```
1  package com.amazonaws.samples;
2
3  import com.amazonaws.services.certificatemanager.AWSCertificateManagerClientBuilder;
4  import com.amazonaws.services.certificatemanager.AWSCertificateManager;
5  import com.amazonaws.services.certificatemanager.model.ListCertificatesRequest;
6  import com.amazonaws.services.certificatemanager.model.ListCertificatesResult;
7
8  import com.amazonaws.auth.profile.ProfileCredentialsProvider;
9  import com.amazonaws.auth.AWSStaticCredentialsProvider;
10 import com.amazonaws.auth.AWSCredentials;
11 import com.amazonaws.regions.Regions;
12
13 import com.amazonaws.AmazonClientException;
14
15 import java.util.Arrays;
16 import java.util.List;
17
18 /**
19  * This sample demonstrates how to use the ListCertificates function in the AWS Certificate
20  * Manager service.
21  *
22  * Input parameters:
23  *    CertificateStatuses - An array of strings that contains the statuses to use for filtering.
24  *    MaxItems - The maximum number of certificates to return in the response.
25  *    NextToken - Use when paginating results.
26  *
27  * Output parameters:
28  *    CertificateSummaryList - A list of certificates.
29  *    NextToken - Use to show additional results when paginating a truncated list.
30  *
31  */
32
33 public class AWSCertificateManagerExample {
34
35     public static void main(String[] args) throws Exception{
36
37         // Retrieve your credentials from the C:\Users\name\.aws\credentials file in Windows
38         // or the ~/.aws/credentials file in Linux.
39         AWSCredentials credentials = null;
40         try {
41             credentials = new ProfileCredentialsProvider().getCredentials();
42         }
43         catch (Exception ex) {
44             throw new AmazonClientException("Cannot load the credentials from file.", ex);
45         }
46
47         // Create a client.
48         AWSCertificateManager client = AWSCertificateManagerClientBuilder.standard()
49                 .withRegion(Regions.US_EAST_1)
50                 .withCredentials(new AWSStaticCredentialsProvider(credentials))
```

```
51          .build();
52
53      // Create a request object and set the parameters.
54      ListCertificatesRequest req = new ListCertificatesRequest();
55      List<String> Statuses = Arrays.asList("ISSUED", "EXPIRED", "PENDING_VALIDATION", "FAILED")
            ;
56      req.setCertificateStatuses(Statuses);
57      req.setMaxItems(10);
58
59      // Retrieve the list of certificates.
60      ListCertificatesResult result = null;
61      try {
62          result = client.listCertificates(req);
63      }
64      catch (Exception ex)
65      {
66          throw ex;
67      }
68
69      // Display the certificate list.
70      System.out.println(result);
71  }
72 }
```

The preceding sample creates output similar to the following.

```
1  {
2      CertificateSummaryList: [{
3          CertificateArn: arn:aws:acm:region:account:certificate
                /12345678-1234-1234-1234-123456789012,
4          DomainName: www.example1.com
5      },
6      {
7          CertificateArn: arn:aws:acm:region:account:certificate
                /12345678-1234-1234-1234-123456789012,
8          DomainName: www.example2.com
9      },
10     {
11         CertificateArn: arn:aws:acm:region:account:certificate
                /12345678-1234-1234-1234-123456789012,
12         DomainName: www.example3.com
13     }]
14 }
```

Listing Tags for a Certificate

The following CloudTrail example shows the results of a call to the ListTagsForCertificate API.

Note

The CloudTrail log for the `ListTagsForCertificate` action does not display your tags. You can view the tag list by using the console, the AWS Command Line Interface, or the ListTagsForCertificate API.

```
1  {
2      Records: [{
3          eventVersion: "1.04",
4          userIdentity: {
5              type: "IAMUser",
6              principalId: "AIDACKCEVSQ6C2EXAMPLE",
7              arn: "arn:aws:iam::123456789012:user/Alice",
8              accountId: "123456789012",
9              accessKeyId: "AKIAIOSFODNN7EXAMPLE",
10             userName: "Alice"
11         },
12         eventTime: "2016-04-06T13:30:11Z",
13         eventSource: "acm.amazonaws.com",
14         eventName: "ListTagsForCertificate",
15         awsRegion: "us-east-1",
16         sourceIPAddress: "192.0.2.0",
17         userAgent: "aws-cli/1.10.16",
18         requestParameters: {
19             certificateArn: "arn:aws:acm:us-east-1:123456789012:certificate
                   /12345678-1234-1234-1234-123456789012"
20         },
21         responseElements: null,
22         requestID: "b010767f-fbfb-11e5-b596-79e9a97a2544",
23         eventID: "32181be6-a4a0-48d3-8014-c0d972b5163b",
24         eventType: "AwsApiCall",
25         recipientAccountId: "123456789012"
26     }]
27  }
```

Removing Tags from a Certificate

The following CloudTrail example shows the results of a call to the RemoveTagsFromCertificate API.

```
1  {
2      Records: [{
3          eventVersion: "1.04",
4          userIdentity: {
5              type: "IAMUser",
6              principalId: "AIDACKCEVSQ6C2EXAMPLE",
7              arn: "arn:aws:iam::123456789012:user/Alice",
8              accountId: "123456789012",
9              accessKeyId: "AKIAIOSFODNN7EXAMPLE",
10             userName: "Alice"
11         },
12         eventTime: "2016-04-06T14:10:01Z",
13         eventSource: "acm.amazonaws.com",
14         eventName: "RemoveTagsFromCertificate",
15         awsRegion: "us-east-1",
16         sourceIPAddress: "192.0.2.0",
17         userAgent: "aws-cli/1.10.16",
18         requestParameters: {
19             certificateArn: "arn:aws:acm:us-east-1:123456789012:certificate
                   /12345678-1234-1234-1234-123456789012",
20             tags: [{
21                 value: "Bob",
22                 key: "Admin"
23             }]
24         },
25         responseElements: null,
26         requestID: "40ded461-fc01-11e5-a747-85804766d6c9",
27         eventID: "0cfa142e-ef74-4b21-9515-47197780c424",
28         eventType: "AwsApiCall",
29         recipientAccountId: "123456789012"
30     }]
31 }
```

Requesting a Certificate

The following example shows how to use the RequestCertificate function.

```
1 package com.amazonaws.samples;
2
3 import com.amazonaws.services.certificatemanager.AWSCertificateManagerClientBuilder;
4 import com.amazonaws.services.certificatemanager.AWSCertificateManager;
5 import com.amazonaws.services.certificatemanager.model.RequestCertificateRequest;
6 import com.amazonaws.services.certificatemanager.model.RequestCertificateResult;
7
8 import com.amazonaws.services.certificatemanager.model.InvalidDomainValidationOptionsException;
9 import com.amazonaws.services.certificatemanager.model.LimitExceededException;
10 import com.amazonaws.AmazonClientException;
11
12 import com.amazonaws.auth.profile.ProfileCredentialsProvider;
13 import com.amazonaws.auth.AWSStaticCredentialsProvider;
14 import com.amazonaws.auth.AWSCredentials;
15 import com.amazonaws.regions.Regions;
16
17 import java.util.ArrayList;
18
19 /**
20  * This sample demonstrates how to use the RequestCertificate function in the AWS Certificate
21  * Manager service.
22  *
23  * Input parameters:
24  *    DomainName - FQDN of your site.
25  *    DomainValidationOptions - Domain name for email validation.
26  *    IdempotencyToken - Distinguishes between calls to RequestCertificate.
27  *    SubjectAlternativeNames - Additional FQDNs for the subject alternative names extension.
28  *
29  * Output parameter:
30  *    Certificate ARN - The Amazon Resource Name (ARN) of the certificate you requested.
31  *
32  */
33
34 public class AWSCertificateManagerExample {
35
36     public static void main(String[] args) {
37
38         // Retrieve your credentials from the C:\Users\name\.aws\credentials file in Windows
39         // or the ~/.aws/credentials file in Linux.
40         AWSCredentials credentials = null;
41         try {
42             credentials = new ProfileCredentialsProvider().getCredentials();
43         }
44         catch (Exception ex) {
45             throw new AmazonClientException("Cannot load your credentials from file.", ex);
46         }
47
48         // Create a client.
49         AWSCertificateManager client = AWSCertificateManagerClientBuilder.standard()
50                 .withRegion(Regions.US_EAST_1)
```

```
51        .withCredentials(new AWSStaticCredentialsProvider(credentials))
52        .build();
53
54    // Specify a SAN.
55    ArrayList<String> san = new ArrayList<String>();
56    san.add("www.example.com");
57
58    // Create a request object and set the input parameters.
59    RequestCertificateRequest req = new RequestCertificateRequest();
60    req.setDomainName("example.com");
61    req.setIdempotencyToken("1Aq25pTy");
62    req.setSubjectAlternativeNames(san);
63
64    // Create a result object and display the certificate ARN.
65    RequestCertificateResult result = null;
66    try {
67        result = client.requestCertificate(req);
68    }
69    catch(InvalidDomainValidationOptionsException ex)
70    {
71        throw ex;
72    }
73    catch(LimitExceededException ex)
74    {
75        throw ex;
76    }
77
78    // Display the ARN.
79    System.out.println(result);
80
81  }
82
83 }
```

The preceding sample creates output similar to the following.

```
1 {CertificateArn: arn:aws:acm:region:account:certificate/12345678-1234-1234-1234-123456789012}
```

Resending Validation Email

The following example shows you how to use the ResendValidationEmail function.

```java
1 package com.amazonaws.samples;
2
3 import com.amazonaws.services.certificatemanager.AWSCertificateManagerClientBuilder;
4 import com.amazonaws.services.certificatemanager.AWSCertificateManager;
5 import com.amazonaws.services.certificatemanager.model.ResendValidationEmailRequest;
6 import com.amazonaws.services.certificatemanager.model.ResendValidationEmailResult;
7
8 import com.amazonaws.services.certificatemanager.model.InvalidDomainValidationOptionsException;
9 import com.amazonaws.services.certificatemanager.model.ResourceNotFoundException;
10 import com.amazonaws.services.certificatemanager.model.InvalidStateException;
11 import com.amazonaws.services.certificatemanager.model.InvalidArnException;
12 import com.amazonaws.AmazonClientException;
13
14 import com.amazonaws.auth.profile.ProfileCredentialsProvider;
15 import com.amazonaws.auth.AWSStaticCredentialsProvider;
16 import com.amazonaws.auth.AWSCredentials;
17 import com.amazonaws.regions.Regions;
18
19 /**
20  * This sample demonstrates how to use the ResendValidationEmail function in the AWS Certificate
21  * Manager service.
22  *
23  * Input parameters:
24  *    CertificateArn - Amazon Resource Name (ARN) of the certificate request.
25  *    Domain - FQDN in the certificate request.
26  *    ValidationDomain - The base validation domain that is used to send email.
27  *
28  */
29
30 public class AWSCertificateManagerExample {
31
32     public static void main(String[] args) {
33
34         // Retrieve your credentials from the C:\Users\name\.aws\credentials file in Windows
35         // or the ~/.aws/credentials file in Linux.
36         AWSCredentials credentials = null;
37         try {
38             credentials = new ProfileCredentialsProvider().getCredentials();
39         }
40         catch (Exception ex) {
41             throw new AmazonClientException("Cannot load your credentials from file.", ex);
42         }
43
44         // Create a client.
45         AWSCertificateManager client = AWSCertificateManagerClientBuilder.standard()
46                 .withRegion(Regions.US_EAST_1)
47                 .withCredentials(new AWSStaticCredentialsProvider(credentials))
48                 .build();
49
50         // Create a request object and set the input parameters.
```

```
51    ResendValidationEmailRequest req = new ResendValidationEmailRequest();
52    req.setCertificateArn("arn:aws:acm:region:account:certificate
          /12345678-1234-1234-1234-123456789012");
53    req.setDomain("gregpe.io");
54    req.setValidationDomain("gregpe.io");
55
56    // Create a result object.
57    ResendValidationEmailResult result = null;
58    try {
59        result = client.resendValidationEmail(req);
60    }
61    catch(ResourceNotFoundException ex)
62    {
63        throw ex;
64    }
65    catch (InvalidStateException ex)
66    {
67        throw ex;
68    }
69    catch (InvalidArnException ex)
70    {
71        throw ex;
72    }
73    catch (InvalidDomainValidationOptionsException ex)
74    {
75        throw ex;
76    }
77
78    // Display the result.
79    System.out.println(result.toString());
80
81  }
82 }
```

The preceding sample resends your validation email and displays an empty set.

```
1 {}
```

Logging ACM-Related API Calls

You can use CloudTrail to audit API calls made by services that are integrated with ACM. For more information about using CloudTrail, see the AWS CloudTrail User Guide. The following examples show the types of logs that can be generated depending on the AWS resources on which you provision the ACM Certificate.

Topics

- Creating a Load Balancer
- Registering an Amazon EC2 Instance with a Load Balancer
- Encrypting a Private Key
- Decrypting a Private Key

Creating a Load Balancer

The following example shows a call to the `CreateLoadBalancer` function by an IAM user named Alice. The name of the load balancer is `TestLinuxDefault`, and the listener is created using an ACM Certificate.

```
1  {
2      "eventVersion": "1.03",
3      "userIdentity": {
4          "type": "IAMUser",
5          "principalId": "AIDACKCEVSQ6C2EXAMPLE",
6          "arn": "arn:aws:iam::111122223333:user/Alice",
7          "accountId": "111122223333",
8          "accessKeyId": "AKIAIOSFODNN7EXAMPLE",
9          "userName": "Alice"
10     },
11     "eventTime": "2016-01-01T21:10:36Z",
12     "eventSource": "elasticloadbalancing.amazonaws.com",
13     "eventName": "CreateLoadBalancer",
14     "awsRegion": "us-east-1",
15     "sourceIPAddress": "192.0.2.0/24",
16     "userAgent": "aws-cli/1.9.15",
17     "requestParameters": {
18         "availabilityZones": ["us-east-1b"],
19         "loadBalancerName": "LinuxTest",
20         "listeners": [{
21             "sSLCertificateId": "arn:aws:acm:us-east-1:111122223333:certificate
                    /12345678-1234-1234-1234-123456789012",
22             "protocol": "HTTPS",
23             "loadBalancerPort": 443,
24             "instanceProtocol": "HTTP",
25             "instancePort": 80
26         }]
27     },
28     "responseElements": {
29         "dNSName": "LinuxTest-1234567890.us-east-1.elb.amazonaws.com"
30     },
31     "requestID": "19669c3b-b0cc-11e5-85b2-57397210a2e5",
32     "eventID": "5d6c00c9-a9b8-46ef-9f3b-4589f5be63f7",
33     "eventType": "AwsApiCall",
34     "recipientAccountId": "111122223333"
35  }
```

Registering an Amazon EC2 Instance with a Load Balancer

When you provision your website or application on an Amazon Elastic Compute Cloud (Amazon EC2) instance, the load balancer must be made aware of that instance. This can be accomplished through the Elastic Load Balancing console or the AWS Command Line Interface. The following example shows a call to RegisterInstancesWithLoadBalancer for a load balancer named LinuxTest on AWS account 123456789012.

```
1  {
2      "eventVersion": "1.03",
3      "userIdentity": {
4          "type": "IAMUser",
5          "principalId": "AIDACKCEVSQ6C2EXAMPLE",
6          "arn": "arn:aws:iam::123456789012:user/ALice",
7          "accountId": "123456789012",
8          "accessKeyId": "AKIAIOSFODNN7EXAMPLE",
9          "userName": "Alice",
10         "sessionContext": {
11             "attributes": {
12                 "mfaAuthenticated": "false",
13                 "creationDate": "2016-01-01T19:35:52Z"
14             }
15         },
16         "invokedBy": "signin.amazonaws.com"
17     },
18     "eventTime": "2016-01-01T21:11:45Z",
19     "eventSource": "elasticloadbalancing.amazonaws.com",
20     "eventName": "RegisterInstancesWithLoadBalancer",
21     "awsRegion": "us-east-1",
22     "sourceIPAddress": "192.0.2.0/24",
23     "userAgent": "signin.amazonaws.com",
24     "requestParameters": {
25         "loadBalancerName": "LinuxTest",
26         "instances": [{
27             "instanceId": "i-c67f4e78"
28         }]
29     },
30     "responseElements": {
31         "instances": [{
32             "instanceId": "i-c67f4e78"
33         }]
34     },
35     "requestID": "438b07dc-b0cc-11e5-8afb-cda7ba020551",
36     "eventID": "9f284ca6-cbe5-42a1-8251-4f0e6b5739d6",
37     "eventType": "AwsApiCall",
38     "recipientAccountId": "123456789012"
39  }
```

Encrypting a Private Key

The following example shows an **Encrypt** call that encrypts the private key associated with an ACM Certificate. Encryption is performed within AWS.

```
1  {
2      "Records": [
3      {
4          "eventVersion": "1.03",
5          "userIdentity": {
6              "type": "IAMUser",
7              "principalId": "AIDACKCEVSQ6C2EXAMPLE",
8              "arn": "arn:aws:iam::111122223333:user/acm",
9              "accountId": "111122223333",
10             "accessKeyId": "AKIAIOSFODNN7EXAMPLE",
11             "userName": "acm"
12         },
13         "eventTime": "2016-01-05T18:36:29Z",
14         "eventSource": "kms.amazonaws.com",
15         "eventName": "Encrypt",
16         "awsRegion": "us-east-1",
17         "sourceIPAddress": "AWS Internal",
18         "userAgent": "aws-internal",
19         "requestParameters": {
20             "keyId": "arn:aws:kms:us-east-1:123456789012:alias/aws/acm",
21             "encryptionContext": {
22                 "aws:acm:arn": "arn:aws:acm:us-east-1:123456789012:certificate
                       /12345678-1234-1234-1234-123456789012"
23             }
24         },
25         "responseElements": null,
26         "requestID": "3c417351-b3db-11e5-9a24-7d9457362fcc",
27         "eventID": "1794fe70-796a-45f5-811b-6584948f24ac",
28         "readOnly": true,
29         "resources": [{
30             "ARN": "arn:aws:kms:us-east-1:123456789012:key
                   /87654321-4321-4321-4321-210987654321",
31             "accountId": "123456789012"
32         }],
33         "eventType": "AwsServiceEvent",
34         "recipientAccountId": "123456789012"
35     }]
36 }
```

Decrypting a Private Key

The following example shows a `Decrypt` call that decrypts the private key associated with an ACM Certificate. Decryption is performed within AWS, and the decrypted key never leaves AWS.

```
1    {
2        "eventVersion": "1.03",
3        "userIdentity": {
4            "type": "AssumedRole",
5            "principalId": "AIDACKCEVSQ6C2EXAMPLE:1aba0dc8b3a728d6998c234a99178eff",
6            "arn": "arn:aws:sts::111122223333:assumed-role/DecryptACMCertificate/1
                 aba0dc8b3a728d6998c234a99178eff",
7            "accountId": "111122223333",
8            "accessKeyId": "AKIAIOSFODNN7EXAMPLE",
9            "sessionContext": {
10               "attributes": {
11                   "mfaAuthenticated": "false",
12                   "creationDate": "2016-01-01T21:13:28Z"
13               },
14               "sessionIssuer": {
15                   "type": "Role",
16                   "principalId": "APKAEIBAERJR2EXAMPLE",
17                   "arn": "arn:aws:iam::111122223333:role/DecryptACMCertificate",
18                   "accountId": "111122223333",
19                   "userName": "DecryptACMCertificate"
20               }
21           }
22       },
23       "eventTime": "2016-01-01T21:13:28Z",
24       "eventSource": "kms.amazonaws.com",
25       "eventName": "Decrypt",
26       "awsRegion": "us-east-1",
27       "sourceIPAddress": "AWS Internal",
28       "userAgent": "aws-internal/3",
29       "requestParameters": {
30           "encryptionContext": {
31               "aws:elasticloadbalancing:arn": "arn:aws:elasticloadbalancing:us-east
                     -1:123456789012:loadbalancer/LinuxTest",
32               "aws:acm:arn": "arn:aws:acm:us-east-1:123456789012:certificate
                     /87654321-4321-4321-4321-210987654321"
33           }
34       },
35       "responseElements": null,
36       "requestID": "809a70ff-b0cc-11e5-8f42-c7fdf1cb6e6a",
37       "eventID": "7f89f7a7-baff-4802-8a88-851488607fb9",
38       "readOnly": true,
39       "resources": [{
40           "ARN": "arn:aws:kms:us-east-1:123456789012:key
                 /12345678-1234-1234-1234-123456789012",
41           "accountId": "123456789012"
42       }],
43       "eventType": "AwsServiceEvent",
44       "recipientAccountId": "123456789012"
45   }
```

Using the ACM API

You can use the AWS Certificate Manager API to interact with the service programmatically by sending HTTP requests. For more information, see the AWS Certificate Manager API Reference.

In addition to the web API (or HTTP API), you can use the AWS SDKs and command line tools to interact with ACM and other services. For more information, see Tools for Amazon Web Services.

The following topics show you how to use one of the AWS SDKs, the AWS SDK for Java, to perform some of the available operations in the AWS Certificate Manager API.

Topics

- Adding Tags to a Certificate
- Deleting a Certificate
- Describing a Certificate
- Exporting a Certificate
- Retrieve a Certificate and Certificate Chain
- Importing a Certificate
- Listing Certificates
- Listing Certificate Tags
- Removing Tags to a Certificate
- Requesting a Certificate
- Resending Validation Email

Exporting a Certificate

The following example shows how to use the ExportCertificate function. The function exports a private certificate issued by a private certificate authority (CA). It also exports the certificate chain and private key. In the example, the passphrase for the key is stored in a local file.

```
1  package com.amazonaws.samples;
2
3  import com.amazonaws.AmazonClientException;
4
5  import com.amazonaws.auth.profile.ProfileCredentialsProvider;
6  import com.amazonaws.auth.AWSStaticCredentialsProvider;
7  import com.amazonaws.auth.AWSCredentials;
8  import com.amazonaws.regions.Regions;
9
10 import com.amazonaws.services.certificatemanager.AWSCertificateManagerClientBuilder;
11 import com.amazonaws.services.certificatemanager.AWSCertificateManager;
12
13
14 import com.amazonaws.services.certificatemanager.model.ExportCertificateRequest;
15 import com.amazonaws.services.certificatemanager.model.ExportCertificateResult;
16
17 import com.amazonaws.services.certificatemanager.model.InvalidArnException;
18 import com.amazonaws.services.certificatemanager.model.InvalidTagException;
19 import com.amazonaws.services.certificatemanager.model.ResourceNotFoundException;
20
21 import java.io.FileNotFoundException;
22 import java.io.IOException;
23 import java.io.RandomAccessFile;
24 import java.nio.ByteBuffer;
25 import java.nio.channels.FileChannel;
26
27 public class ExportCertificate {
28
29    public static void main(String[] args) throws Exception {
30
31        // Retrieve your credentials from the C:\Users\name\.aws\credentials file in Windows
32        // or the ~/.aws/credentials in Linux.
33        AWSCredentials credentials = null;
34        try {
35            credentials = new ProfileCredentialsProvider().getCredentials();
36        }
37        catch (Exception ex) {
38            throw new AmazonClientException("Cannot load your credentials from file.", ex);
39        }
40
41        // Create a client.
42        AWSCertificateManager client = AWSCertificateManagerClientBuilder.standard()
43                .withRegion(Regions.your_region)
44                .withCredentials(new AWSStaticCredentialsProvider(credentials))
45                .build();
46
47        // Initialize a file descriptor for the passphrase file.
48        RandomAccessFile file_passphrase = null;
```

```
49
50      // Initialize a buffer for the passphrase.
51      ByteBuffer buf_passphrase = null;
52
53      // Create a file stream for reading the private key passphrase.
54      try {
55          file_passphrase = new RandomAccessFile("C:\\Temp\\password.txt", "r");
56      }
57      catch (IllegalArgumentException ex) {
58          throw ex;
59      }
60      catch (SecurityException ex) {
61          throw ex;
62      }
63      catch (FileNotFoundException ex) {
64          throw ex;
65      }
66
67      // Create a channel to map the file.
68      FileChannel channel_passphrase = file_passphrase.getChannel();
69
70      // Map the file to the buffer.
71      try {
72          buf_passphrase = channel_passphrase.map(FileChannel.MapMode.READ_ONLY, 0,
                channel_passphrase.size());
73
74          // Clean up after the file is mapped.
75          channel_passphrase.close();
76          file_passphrase.close();
77      }
78      catch (IOException ex)
79      {
80          throw ex;
81      }
82
83      // Create a request object.
84      ExportCertificateRequest req = new ExportCertificateRequest();
85
86      // Set the certificate ARN.
87      req.withCertificateArn("arn:aws:acm:region:account:"
88              +"certificate/M12345678-1234-1234-1234-123456789012");
89
90      // Set the passphrase.
91      req.withPassphrase(buf_passphrase);
92
93      // Export the certificate.
94      ExportCertificateResult result = null;
95
96      try {
97          result = client.exportCertificate(req);
98      }
99      catch(InvalidArnException ex)
100     {
101         throw ex;
```

113

```
102         }
103         catch (InvalidTagException ex)
104         {
105             throw ex;
106         }
107         catch (ResourceNotFoundException ex)
108         {
109             throw ex;
110         }
111
112         // Clear the buffer.
113         buf_passphrase.clear();
114
115         // Display the certificate and certificate chain.
116         String certificate = result.getCertificate();
117         System.out.println(certificate);
118
119         String certificate_chain = result.getCertificateChain();
120         System.out.println(certificate_chain);
121
122         // This example retrieves but does not display the private key.
123         String private_key = result.getPrivateKey();
124     }
125 }
```

Retrieve a Certificate and Certificate Chain

The following example shows how to use the GetCertificate function.

```
1 package com.amazonaws.samples;
2
3 import com.amazonaws.regions.Regions;
4 import com.amazonaws.services.certificatemanager.AWSCertificateManagerClientBuilder;
5 import com.amazonaws.services.certificatemanager.AWSCertificateManager;
6 import com.amazonaws.services.certificatemanager.model.GetCertificateRequest;
7 import com.amazonaws.services.certificatemanager.model.GetCertificateResult;
8
9 import com.amazonaws.auth.profile.ProfileCredentialsProvider;
10 import com.amazonaws.auth.AWSStaticCredentialsProvider;
11 import com.amazonaws.auth.AWSCredentials;
12
13 import com.amazonaws.services.certificatemanager.model.InvalidArnException;
14 import com.amazonaws.services.certificatemanager.model.ResourceNotFoundException;
15 import com.amazonaws.services.certificatemanager.model.RequestInProgressException;
16 import com.amazonaws.AmazonClientException;
17
18 /**
19 * This sample demonstrates how to use the GetCertificate function in the AWS Certificate
20 * Manager service.
21 *
22 * Input parameter:
23 *    CertificateArn - The ARN of the certificate to retrieve.
24 *
25 * Output parameters:
26 *    Certificate - A base64-encoded certificate in PEM format.
27 *    CertificateChain - The base64-encoded certificate chain in PEM format.
28 *
29 */
30
31 public class AWSCertificateManagerExample {
32
33     public static void main(String[] args) throws Exception{
34
35         // Retrieve your credentials from the C:\Users\name\.aws\credentials file in Windows
36         // or the ~/.aws/credentials file in Linux.
37         AWSCredentials credentials = null;
38         try {
39             credentials = new ProfileCredentialsProvider().getCredentials();
40         }
41         catch (Exception ex) {
42             throw new AmazonClientException("Cannot load the credentials from the credential
                    profiles file.", ex);
43         }
44
45         // Create a client.
46         AWSCertificateManager client = AWSCertificateManagerClientBuilder.standard()
47                 .withRegion(Regions.US_EAST_1)
48                 .withCredentials(new AWSStaticCredentialsProvider(credentials))
49                 .build();
```

```
50
51      // Create a request object and set the ARN of the certificate to be described.
52      GetCertificateRequest req = new GetCertificateRequest();
53      req.setCertificateArn("arn:aws:acm:region:account:certificate
           /12345678-1234-1234-1234-123456789012");
54
55      // Retrieve the certificate and certificate chain.
56      // If you recently requested the certificate, loop until it has been created.
57      GetCertificateResult result = null;
58      long totalTimeout = 1200001;
59      long timeSlept = 01;
60      long sleepInterval = 100001;
61      while (result == null && timeSlept < totalTimeout) {
62          try {
63              result = client.getCertificate(req);
64          }
65          catch (RequestInProgressException ex) {
66              Thread.sleep(sleepInterval);
67          }
68          catch (ResourceNotFoundException ex)
69          {
70              throw ex;
71          }
72          catch (InvalidArnException ex)
73          {
74              throw ex;
75          }
76
77          timeSlept += sleepInterval;
78      }
79
80      // Display the certificate information.
81      System.out.println(result);
82    }
83  }
```

The preceding example creates output similar to the following.

```
1  {Certificate: -----BEGIN CERTIFICATE-----
2     base64-encoded certificate
3  -----END CERTIFICATE-----,
4  CertificateChain: -----BEGIN CERTIFICATE-----
5     base64-encoded certificate chain
6  -----END CERTIFICATE-----
7  }
```

Importing a Certificate

The following example shows how to use the ImportCertificate function.

```
1  package com.amazonaws.samples;
2
3  import com.amazonaws.services.certificatemanager.AWSCertificateManagerClientBuilder;
4  import com.amazonaws.services.certificatemanager.AWSCertificateManager;
5
6  import com.amazonaws.auth.profile.ProfileCredentialsProvider;
7  import com.amazonaws.auth.AWSStaticCredentialsProvider;
8  import com.amazonaws.auth.AWSCredentials;
9  import com.amazonaws.regions.Regions;
10
11  import com.amazonaws.services.certificatemanager.model.ImportCertificateRequest;
12  import com.amazonaws.services.certificatemanager.model.ImportCertificateResult;
13  import com.amazonaws.services.certificatemanager.model.LimitExceededException;
14  import com.amazonaws.services.certificatemanager.model.ResourceNotFoundException;
15  import com.amazonaws.AmazonClientException;
16  import java.io.FileNotFoundException;
17  import java.io.IOException;
18
19  import java.io.RandomAccessFile;
20  import java.nio.ByteBuffer;
21  import java.nio.channels.FileChannel;
22
23  /**
24   * This sample demonstrates how to use the ImportCertificate function in the AWS Certificate
           Manager
25   * service.
26   *
27   * Input parameters:
28   *    Certificate - PEM file that contains the certificate to import.
29   *    CertificateArn - Use to reimport a certificate (not included in this example).
30   *    CertificateChain - The certificate chain, not including the end-entity certificate.
31   *    PrivateKey - The private key that matches the public key in the certificate.
32   *
33   * Output parameter:
34   *    CertificcateArn - The ARN of the imported certificate.
35   *
36   */
37  public class AWSCertificateManagerSample {
38
39      public static void main(String[] args) throws Exception {
40
41          // Retrieve your credentials from the C:\Users\name\.aws\credentials file in Windows
42          // or the ~/.aws/credentials file in Linux.
43          AWSCredentials credentials = null;
44          try {
45              credentials = new ProfileCredentialsProvider().getCredentials();
46          }
47          catch (Exception ex) {
48              throw new AmazonClientException(
49                  "Cannot load the credentials from file.", ex);
```

```
50          }
51
52          // Create a client.
53          AWSCertificateManager client = AWSCertificateManagerClientBuilder.standard()
54                  .withRegion(Regions.US_EAST_1)
55                  .withCredentials(new AWSStaticCredentialsProvider(credentials))
56                  .build();
57
58          // Initialize the file descriptors.
59          RandomAccessFile file_certificate = null;
60          RandomAccessFile file_chain = null;
61          RandomAccessFile file_key = null;
62
63          // Initialize the buffers.
64          ByteBuffer buf_certificate = null;
65          ByteBuffer buf_chain = null;
66          ByteBuffer buf_key = null;
67
68          // Create the file streams for reading.
69          try {
70              file_certificate = new RandomAccessFile("C:\\Temp\\certificate.pem", "r");
71              file_chain = new RandomAccessFile("C:\\Temp\\chain.pem", "r");
72              file_key = new RandomAccessFile("C:\\Temp\\private_key.pem", "r");
73          }
74          catch (IllegalArgumentException ex) {
75              throw ex;
76          }
77          catch (SecurityException ex) {
78              throw ex;
79          }
80          catch (FileNotFoundException ex) {
81              throw ex;
82          }
83
84          // Create channels for mapping the files.
85          FileChannel channel_certificate = file_certificate.getChannel();
86          FileChannel channel_chain = file_chain.getChannel();
87          FileChannel channel_key = file_key.getChannel();
88
89          // Map the files to buffers.
90          try {
91              buf_certificate = channel_certificate.map(FileChannel.MapMode.READ_ONLY, 0,
92                  channel_certificate.size());
                buf_chain = channel_chain.map(FileChannel.MapMode.READ_ONLY, 0, channel_chain.size());
93              buf_key = channel_key.map(FileChannel.MapMode.READ_ONLY, 0, channel_key.size());
94
95              // The files have been mapped, so clean up.
96              channel_certificate.close();
97              channel_chain.close();
98              channel_key.close();
99              file_certificate.close();
100             file_chain.close();
101             file_key.close();
102         }
```

```
103    catch (IOException ex)
104    {
105        throw ex;
106    }
107
108    // Create a request object and set the parameters.
109    ImportCertificateRequest req = new ImportCertificateRequest();
110    req.setCertificate(buf_certificate);
111    req.setCertificateChain(buf_chain);
112    req.setPrivateKey(buf_key);
113
114    // Import the certificate.
115    ImportCertificateResult result = null;
116    try {
117        result = client.importCertificate(req);
118    }
119    catch(LimitExceededException ex)
120    {
121        throw ex;
122    }
123    catch (ResourceNotFoundException ex)
124    {
125        throw ex;
126    }
127
128    // Clear the buffers.
129    buf_certificate.clear();
130    buf_chain.clear();
131    buf_key.clear();
132
133    // Retrieve and display the certificate ARN.
134    String arn = result.getCertificateArn();
135    System.out.println(arn);
136    }
137 }
```

Listing Certificate Tags

The following example shows how to use the ListTagsForCertificate function.

```
1  package com.amazonaws.samples;
2
3  import com.amazonaws.services.certificatemanager.AWSCertificateManagerClientBuilder;
4  import com.amazonaws.services.certificatemanager.AWSCertificateManager;
5  import com.amazonaws.services.certificatemanager.model.ListTagsForCertificateRequest;
6  import com.amazonaws.services.certificatemanager.model.ListTagsForCertificateResult;
7
8  import com.amazonaws.services.certificatemanager.model.InvalidArnException;
9  import com.amazonaws.services.certificatemanager.model.ResourceNotFoundException;
10 import com.amazonaws.AmazonClientException;
11
12 import com.amazonaws.auth.AWSCredentials;
13 import com.amazonaws.auth.profile.ProfileCredentialsProvider;
14 import com.amazonaws.auth.AWSStaticCredentialsProvider;
15 import com.amazonaws.regions.Regions;
16
17
18 /**
19  * This sample demonstrates how to use the ListTagsForCertificate function in the AWS
        Certificate
20  * Manager service.
21  *
22  * Input parameter:
23  *    CertificateArn - The ARN of the certificate whose tags you want to list.
24  *
25  */
26
27 public class AWSCertificateManagerExample {
28
29     public static void main(String[] args) throws Exception{
30
31         // Retrieve your credentials from the C:\Users\name\.aws\credentials file in Windows
32         // or the ~/.aws/credentials file in Linux.
33         AWSCredentials credentials = null;
34         try {
35             credentials = new ProfileCredentialsProvider().getCredentials();
36         }
37         catch (Exception ex) {
38             throw new AmazonClientException("Cannot load your credentials from file.", ex);
39         }
40
41         // Create a client.
42         AWSCertificateManager client = AWSCertificateManagerClientBuilder.standard()
43                 .withRegion(Regions.US_EAST_1)
44                 .withCredentials(new AWSStaticCredentialsProvider(credentials))
45                 .build();
46
47         // Create a request object and specify the ARN of the certificate.
48         ListTagsForCertificateRequest req = new ListTagsForCertificateRequest();
```

```
49    req.setCertificateArn("arn:aws:acm:region:account:certificate
         /12345678-1234-1234-1234-123456789012");
50
51    // Create a result object.
52    ListTagsForCertificateResult result = null;
53    try {
54        result = client.listTagsForCertificate(req);
55    }
56    catch(InvalidArnException ex) {
57        throw ex;
58    }
59    catch(ResourceNotFoundException ex) {
60        throw ex;
61    }
62
63    // Display the result.
64    System.out.println(result);
65
66    }
67 }
```

The preceding sample creates output similar to the following.

```
1 {Tags: [{Key: Purpose,Value: Test}, {Key: Short_Name,Value: My_Cert}]}
```

Removing Tags to a Certificate

The following example shows how to use the RemoveTagsFromCertificate function.

```
1  package com.amazonaws.samples;
2
3  import com.amazonaws.services.certificatemanager.AWSCertificateManagerClientBuilder;
4  import com.amazonaws.services.certificatemanager.AWSCertificateManager;
5  import com.amazonaws.services.certificatemanager.model.RemoveTagsFromCertificateRequest;
6  import com.amazonaws.services.certificatemanager.model.RemoveTagsFromCertificateResult;
7  import com.amazonaws.services.certificatemanager.model.Tag;
8
9  import com.amazonaws.services.certificatemanager.model.InvalidArnException;
10 import com.amazonaws.services.certificatemanager.model.InvalidTagException;
11 import com.amazonaws.services.certificatemanager.model.ResourceNotFoundException;
12 import com.amazonaws.AmazonClientException;
13
14 import com.amazonaws.auth.profile.ProfileCredentialsProvider;
15 import com.amazonaws.auth.AWSStaticCredentialsProvider;
16 import com.amazonaws.auth.AWSCredentials;
17 import com.amazonaws.regions.Regions;
18
19 import java.util.ArrayList;
20
21 /**
22  * This sample demonstrates how to use the RemoveTagsFromCertificate function in the AWS
         Certificate
23  * Manager service.
24  *
25  * Input parameters:
26  *   CertificateArn - The ARN of the certificate from which you want to remove one or more tags.
27  *   Tags - A collection of key-value pairs that specify which tags to remove.
28  *
29  */
30
31 public class AWSCertificateManagerExample {
32
33     public static void main(String[] args) throws Exception {
34
35         // Retrieve your credentials from the C:\Users\name\.aws\credentials file in Windows
36         // or the ~/.aws/credentials file in Linux.
37         AWSCredentials credentials = null;
38         try {
39             credentials = new ProfileCredentialsProvider().getCredentials();
40         }
41         catch (Exception ex) {
42             throw new AmazonClientException("Cannot load your credentials from file.", ex);
43         }
44
45         // Create a client.
46         AWSCertificateManager client = AWSCertificateManagerClientBuilder.standard()
47                 .withRegion(Regions.US_EAST_1)
48                 .withCredentials(new AWSStaticCredentialsProvider(credentials))
49                 .build();
```

```java
50
51      // Specify the tags to remove.
52      Tag tag1 = new Tag();
53      tag1.setKey("Short_Name");
54      tag1.setValue("My_Cert");
55
56      Tag tag2 = new Tag()
57              .withKey("Purpose")
58              .withValue("Test");
59
60      // Add the tags to a collection.
61      ArrayList<Tag> tags = new ArrayList<Tag>();
62      tags.add(tag1);
63      tags.add(tag2);
64
65      // Create a request object.
66      RemoveTagsFromCertificateRequest req = new RemoveTagsFromCertificateRequest();
67      req.setCertificateArn("arn:aws:acm:region:account:certificate
                /12345678-1234-1234-1234-123456789012");
68      req.setTags(tags);
69
70      // Create a result object.
71      RemoveTagsFromCertificateResult result = null;
72      try {
73          result = client.removeTagsFromCertificate(req);
74      }
75      catch(InvalidArnException ex)
76      {
77          throw ex;
78      }
79      catch(InvalidTagException ex)
80      {
81          throw ex;
82      }
83      catch(ResourceNotFoundException ex)
84      {
85          throw ex;
86      }
87
88      // Display the result.
89      System.out.println(result);
90  }
91 }
```

ACM Private Key Security

When you request a public certificate, AWS Certificate Manager (ACM) generates a public/private key pair. For imported certificates, you generate the key pair. The public key becomes part of the certificate. ACM stores the certificate and its corresponding private key, and uses AWS Key Management Service (AWS KMS) to help protect the private key. The process works like this:

1. The first time you request or import a certificate in an AWS region, ACM creates an AWS-managed customer master key (CMK) in AWS KMS with the alias **aws/acm**. This CMK is unique in each AWS account and each AWS region.

2. ACM uses this CMK to encrypt the certificate's private key. ACM stores only an encrypted version of the private key (ACM does not store the private key in plaintext form). ACM uses the same CMK to encrypt the private keys for all certificates in a specific AWS account and a specific AWS region.

3. When you associate the certificate with a service that is integrated with AWS Certificate Manager, ACM sends the certificate and the encrypted private key to the service. You also implicitly create a grant in AWS KMS that allows the service to use the CMK in AWS KMS to decrypt the certificate's private key. For more information about grants, see Using Grants in the *AWS Key Management Service Developer Guide*. For more information about services supported by ACM, see Services Integrated with AWS Certificate Manager.

4. Integrated services use the CMK in AWS KMS to decrypt the private key. Then the service uses the certificate and the decrypted (plaintext) private key to establish secure communication channels (SSL/TLS sessions) with its clients.

5. When the certificate is disassociated from an integrated service, the grant created in step 3 is retired. This means the service can no longer use the CMK in AWS KMS to decrypt the certificate's private key.

Troubleshooting

Consult the following topics if you encounter problems using AWS Certificate Manager.

Topics

- Troubleshoot Certification Authority Authorization (CAA) Problems
- Troubleshoot Email Problems
- Troubleshoot Certificate Importing Problems
- Troubleshoot Certificate Pinning Problems
- Troubleshoot Certificate Request Problems
- Troubleshoot Managed Certificate Renewal Problems
- Troubleshoot Certificate Validation Problems
- Troubleshoot .IO Domain Problems
- Troubleshoot API Gateway Problems

Troubleshoot Certification Authority Authorization (CAA) Problems

You can use CAA DNS records to specify that the Amazon certificate authority (CA) can issue ACM Certificates for your domain or subdomain. If you receive an error during certificate issuance that says **One or more domain names have failed validation due to a Certification Authority Authentication (CAA) error**, check your CAA DNS records. If you receive this error after your ACM Certificate request has been successfully validated, you must update your CAA records and request a certificate again. The **value** field in at least one of your CAA records must contain one the following domain names:

- amazon.com
- amazontrust.com
- awstrust.com
- amazonaws.com

If you do not want ACM to perform CAA checking, do not configure a CAA record for your domain or leave your CAA records blank. For more information about creating a CAA record, see (Optional) Configure a CAA Record.

Troubleshoot Email Problems

Consult the following topics if you have trouble with validation email.

Topics

- Not Receiving Validation Email
- Email Sent to Subdomain
- Hidden Contact Information
- Certificate Renewals
- WHOIS Throttling

Not Receiving Validation Email

When you request a certificate from ACM and choose email validation, domain validation email is sent to three contact addresses specified in WHOIS and to five common administrative addresses. For more information, see Use Email to Validate Domain Ownership. If you are experiencing problems receiving validation email, review the suggestions that follow.

Where to look for email

Validation email is sent to contact addresses listed in WHOIS and to common administrative addresses for the domain. Email is not sent to the AWS account owner unless the owner is also listed as a domain contact in WHOIS. Review the list of email addresses that are displayed in the ACM console (or returned from the CLI or API) to determine where you should be looking for validation email. To see the list, click the icon next to the domain name in the box labeled **Validation not complete**.

The email is marked as spam

Check your spam folder for the validation email.

GMail automatically sorts your email

If you are using GMail, the validation email may have been automatically sorted into the **Updates** or **Promotions** tabs.

The domain registrar does not display contact information or privacy protection is enabled

In some cases, the domain registrant, technical, and administrative contacts in WHOIS may not be publicly available, and AWS therefore cannot reach these contacts. At your discretion, you can choose to configure your registrar to list your email address in WHOIS, although not all registrars support this option. You may be required to make a change directly at your domain's registry. In other cases, the domain contact information may be using a privacy address, such as those provided through WhoisGuard or PrivacyGuard.

For domains purchased from Route 53, privacy protection is enabled by default and your email address is mapped to a `whoisprivacyservice.org` or `contact.gandi.net` email address. Ensure that your registrant email address on file with your domain registrar is up to date so that the email sent to these obscured email addresses can be forwarded to an email address that you control.

Privacy protection for some domains that your purchase with Route 53 will be enabled even if you choose to make your contact information public. For example, privacy protection for the .ca top level domain cannot be programmatically disabled by Route 53. You must contact the AWS Support Center and request that privacy protection be disabled. If email contact information for your domain is not available through WHOIS, or if email sent to the contact information does not reach the domain owner or an authorized representative, we recommend that you configure your domain or subdomain to receive email sent to one or more of the common administrative addresses formed by prepending admin@, administrator@, hostmaster@, webmaster@, and postmaster@ to the requested domain name. For more information about configuring email for your domain, see the documentation for your email service provider and follow the instructions at (Optional) Configure Email for Your Domain. If you are using Amazon WorkMail, see Working with Users in the Amazon WorkMail Administrator Guide.

After making available at least one of the eight email addresses to which AWS sends validation email and confirming that you can receive email for that address, you are ready to request a certificate through ACM. After you make a certificate request, ensure the intended email address appears in the list of email addresses in the AWS Management Console. While the certificate is in the **Pending validation** state, you can expand the list to view it by clicking the icon next to the domain name in the box labeled **Validation not complete**. You can also view the list in **Step 3: Validate** of the ACM **Request a Certificate** wizard. The listed email addresses are the ones to which email was sent.

Missing or incorrectly configured MX records
An MX record is a resource record in the Domain Name System (DNS) database that specifies one or more mail servers that accept email messages for your domain. If your MX record is missing or misconfigured, email can not be sent to any of the five common system administration addresses specified at Use Email to Validate Domain Ownership. Fix your missing or misconfigured MX record and try to resend the email or request your certificate again.

Currently, we recommend that you wait at least one hour before attempting to resend the email or requesting your certificate. To bypass requiring an MX record, you can use the `ValidationDomain` option in the RequestCertificate API or the request-certificate AWS CLI command to specify the domain name to which ACM sends validation emails. If you use the API or the AWS CLI, AWS does not perform an MX lookup.

Contact the Support Center
If, after reviewing the preceding guidance, you still don't receive the domain validation email, please visit the AWS Support Center and create a case. If you don't have a support agreement, post a message to the ACM Discussion Forum.

Email Sent to Subdomain

If you are using the console and request a certificate for a subdomain name such as `sub.test.example.com`, then ACM checks to see if there is an MX record for `sub.test.example.com`. If not, then the parent domain `test.example.com` is checked, and so on, up to the base domain `example.com`. If an MX record is found, the search stops and a validation email is sent to the common administration addresses for the subdomain. So for example, if an MX record is found for `test.example.com`, email is sent to admin@test.example.com, administrator@test.example.com, and the other administrative addresses specified in Use Email to Validate Domain Ownership. If an MX record is not found in any of the subdomains, email is sent to the subdomain that you originally requested the certificate for. For a thorough discussion of how to setup your email and how ACM works with DNS and the WHOIS database, see (Optional) Configure Email for Your Domain.

Instead of using the console, you can use the `ValidationDomain` option in the RequestCertificate API or the request-certificate AWS CLI command to specify the domain name to which ACM sends validation emails. If you use the API or the AWS CLI, AWS does not perform an MX lookup.

Hidden Contact Information

A common problem occurs when you attempt to create a new certificate. Some registrars allow you to hide your contact information in your WHOIS listing. Others allow you to substitute your real email address with a privacy (or proxy) address. This prevents you from receiving validation email at your registered contact addresses.

To receive mail, ensure that your contact information is public in WHOIS, or if your WHOIS listing shows a privacy email address, ensure that email sent to the privacy address is forwarded to your real email address. After your WHOIS setup is complete and as long as your certificate request has not timed out, you can choose to resend the validation email. ACM performs a new WHOIS/MX lookup and sends validation email to your now public contact address.

Certificate Renewals

If you made your WHOIS information public when you requested a new certificate and then later obfuscated your information, ACM cannot retrieve your registered contact addresses when you attempt to renew your certificate. ACM sends validation email to these contact addresses and to five common administrative addresses formed by using your MX record. To address this problem, make your WHOIS information public again and resend the validation emails. ACM performs a new WHOIS/MX lookup and sends validation email to your now public contact addresses.

WHOIS Throttling

Sometimes ACM is unable to contact the WHOIS server even after you have sent multiple requests for validation email. This problem is external to AWS. That is, AWS does not control the WHOIS servers and cannot prevent WHOIS server throttling. If you experience this problem, create a case at the AWS Support Center for help with a workaround.

Troubleshoot Certificate Importing Problems

You can import third party certificates into ACM and associate them with integrated services. If you encounter problems, review the prerequisites and certificate format topics. In particular, note the following:

- You can import only X.509 version 3 SSL/TLS certificates.
- Your certificate can be self–signed or it can be signed by a certificate authority (CA).
- If your certificate is signed by a CA, you must include a certificate chain that chains up to the root of authority.
- Do not include your certificate in the certificate chain.
- Each certificate in the chain must directly certify the one preceding.
- Your certificate, private key, and certificate chain must be PEM–encoded.
- Your private key must not be encrypted.
- Services integrated with ACM allow only algorithms and key sizes they support to be associated with their resources. Support can change. See the documentation for each service to make sure your certificate will work.
- Certificate support by integrated services might differ depending on whether the certificate is imported into IAM or into ACM.
- The certificate must be valid when it is imported.
- Detail information for all of your certificates is displayed in the console. By default, however, if you call the ListCertificates API or the list-certificates AWS CLI command without specifying the `keyTypes` filter, only `RSA_1024` or `RSA_2048` certificates are displayed.

Troubleshoot Certificate Pinning Problems

To renew a certificate, ACM generates a new public-private key pair. If your application uses Certificate Pinning, sometimes known as SSL pinning, to pin an ACM Certificate, the application might not be able to connect to your domain after AWS renews the certificate. For this reason, we recommend that you don't pin an ACM Certificate. If your application must pin a certificate, you can do the following:

- Import your own certificate into ACM and then pin your application to the imported certificate. ACM doesn't provide managed renewal for imported certificates.
- Pin your application to an Amazon root certificate.

Troubleshoot Certificate Request Problems

Consult the following topics if you have trouble requesting an ACM Certificate.

Topics

- Certificate Request Timed Out
- Certificate Request Failed

Certificate Request Timed Out

Requests for ACM Certificates time out if they are not validated within 72 hours. To correct this condition, delete your request and choose **Request a certificate** to begin again. You can use DNS validation or email validation to assert that you own or control the domains listed in your request. We recommend that you use DNS. For more information see, Use DNS to Validate Domain Ownership.

Certificate Request Failed

A request for an ACM Certificate can fail. If that happens, the following explanations can help you understand why the request failed and suggest steps you can take to fix the problem.

Topics

- No Available Contacts
- Domain Not Allowed
- Additional Verification Required
- Invalid Public Domain
- Other

No Available Contacts

You chose email validation when requesting a certificate, but ACM could not find an email address to use for validating one or more of the domain names in the request. To correct this problem, you can do one of the following:

- Ensure that you have a working email address that is registered in WHOIS and that the address is visible when performing a standard WHOIS lookup for the domain names in the certificate request. Typically, you do this through your domain registrar.
- Ensure your domain is configured to receive email. Your domain's name server must have a mail exchanger record (MX record) so ACM's email servers know where to send the domain validation email.

Accomplishing one of the preceding tasks is enough to correct this problem; you don't need to do both. After you correct the problem, request a new certificate. You cannot resubmit a failed certificate request.

For more information about how to ensure that you receive domain validation emails from ACM, see (Optional) Configure Email for Your Domain or Not Receiving Validation Email. If you follow these steps and continue to get the **No Available Contacts** message, then report this to AWS so that we can investigate it.

Domain Not Allowed

ACM did not allow you to request a certificate for one or more of the domain names you specified. Typically, this is because one or more of the domain names in the certificate request was found in the Google Safe Browsing list of unsafe websites or the PhishTank list of valid phishes. To correct this problem, you can do the following:

- Search for your domain name at the Google Safe Browsing Site Status website. If your domain is considered unsafe, see Google Help for Hacked Websites to learn what you can do. If you think your domain is safe, see Request a review to request a review from Google.
- Search for your domain name on the PhishTank home page. If your domain is considered a phish, see Google Help for Hacked Websites or StopBadware Webmaster Help to learn what you can do. If you think your domain is safe, see the PhishTank FAQ for information about how to report a false positive.

After you correct the problem, request a new certificate. You cannot resubmit a failed certificate request.

Additional Verification Required

ACM requires additional information to process this certificate request. To provide this information, use the Support Center to contact AWS Support. If you don't have a support plan, post a new thread in the AWS Certificate Manager discussion forum.

Note
You cannot request a certificate for Amazon-owned domain names such as those ending in amazonaws.com, cloudfront.net, or elasticbeanstalk.com.

Invalid Public Domain

One or more of the domain names in the certificate request is not valid. Typically, this is because a domain name in the request is not a valid top-level domain. Try to request a certificate again, correcting any spelling errors or typos that were in the failed request, and ensuring that all domain names in the request are for valid top-level domains. For example, you cannot request an ACM Certificate for example.invalidpublicdomain because "invalidpublicdomain" is not a valid top-level domain. If you continue to receive this failure reason, contact the Support Center. If you don't have a support plan, post a new thread in the AWS Certificate Manager discussion forum.

Other

Typically, this failure occurs when there is a typographical error in one or more of the domain names in the certificate request. Try to request a certificate again, correcting any spelling errors or typos that were in the failed request. If you continue to receive this failure reason, use the Support Center to contact AWS Support. If you don't have a support plan, post a new thread in the AWS Certificate Manager discussion forum.

Troubleshoot Managed Certificate Renewal Problems

ACM tries to automatically renew your ACM Certificates before they expire so that no action is required from you. Consult the following topics if you have trouble with Managed Renewal for ACM's Amazon-Issued Certificates.

Topics

- Automatic Domain Validation
- Asynchronous Process

Automatic Domain Validation

Before ACM can renew your certificates automatically, the following must be true:

- ACM must be able to establish an HTTPS connection with each domain in the certificate.
- For each connection, the certificate that is returned must match the one that ACM is renewing.
- Your certificate must be associated with an AWS service that is integrated with ACM.
- ACM must be able to validate each domain name listed in your certificate.

To increase the likelihood that ACM can renew your certificate automatically, do the following:

Use the certificate with an AWS resource
Make sure that your certificate is in use with a supported AWS resource. For information about the resources that ACM supports, see Services Integrated with AWS Certificate Manager.

Configure the resource to accept HTTPS requests from the Internet
Make sure that the AWS resource that has your ACM Certificate is configured to accept HTTPS requests from the internet.

Configure DNS to route your domain name to the resource that hosts your ACM Certificate
Make sure that HTTPS requests to the domain names in your certificate are routed to the resource that has your certificate.

Asynchronous Process

Managed Renewal for ACM's Amazon-Issued Certificates is an asynchronous process. This means that the steps don't occur in immediate succession. After all domain names in an ACM Certificate have been validated, there might be a delay before ACM obtains the new certificate. An additional delay can occur between the time when ACM obtains the renewed certificate and the time when that certificate is deployed to the AWS resources that use it. Therefore, changes to the certificate status can take up to several hours to appear in the console.

Troubleshoot Certificate Validation Problems

Consult the following topic if your validation appears to be stuck in a pending state.

Validation Not Complete

If the ACM Certificate request status is **Pending validation**, the request is waiting for action from you. If you chose email validation when you made the request, you or an authorized representative must respond to the validation email messages. These messages were sent to the registered WHOIS contact addresses and other common email addresses for the requested domain. For more information, see Use Email to Validate Domain Ownership. If you chose DNS validation, you must write the CNAME record that ACM created for you to your DNS database. For more information, see Use DNS to Validate Domain Ownership.

Important
You must validate that you own or control every domain name that you included in your certificate request. If you chose email validation, you will receive validation email messages for each domain. If you do not, then see Not Receiving Validation Email. If you chose DNS validation, you must create one CNAME record for each domain.

We recommend that you use DNS validation rather than email validation.

Troubleshoot .IO Domain Problems

The .IO domain is assigned to the British Indian Ocean Territory. Currently, the domain registry does not display your public information from the WHOIS database. This is true whether you have privacy protection for the domain enabled or disabled. When a WHOIS lookup is performed, only obfuscated registrar information is returned. Therefore, ACM is unable to send validation email to the following three registered contact addresses that are usually available in WHOIS.

- Domain registrant
- Technical contact
- Administrative contact

ACM does, however, send validation email to the following five common system addresses where *your_domain* is the domain name you entered when you initially requested a certificate and `.io` is the top level domain.

- administrator@*your_domain*.io
- hostmaster@*your_domain*.io
- postmaster@*your_domain*.io
- webmaster@*your_domain*.io
- admin@*your_domain*.io

To receive validation mail for an .IO domain, make sure that you have one of the preceding five email accounts enabled. If you do not, you will not receive validation email and you will not be issued an ACM certificate.

Note
We recommend that you use DNS validation rather than email validation. For more information, see Use DNS to Validate Domain Ownership.

Troubleshoot API Gateway Problems

When you deploy an *edge-optimized* API endpoint, API Gateway sets up a CloudFront distribution for you. The CloudFront distribution is owned by API Gateway, not by your account. The distribution is bound to the ACM Certificate that you used when deploying your API. To remove the binding and allow ACM to delete your certificate, you must remove the API Gateway custom domain that is associated with the certificate.

When you deploy a *regional* API endpoint, API Gateway creates an application load balancer (ALB) on your behalf. The load balancer is owned by API Gateway and is not visible to you. The ALB is bound to the ACM Certificate that you used when deploying your API. To remove the binding and allow ACM to delete your certificate, you must remove the API Gateway custom domain that is associated with the certificate.

Document History

The following table describes the documentation release history of AWS Certificate Manager.

Latest documentation update: March 27, 2018

Change	Description	Release Date
New content	Added certificate transparency logging to Opting Out of Certificate Transparency Logging and Certificate Transparency Logging.	March 27, 2018
New content	Added DNS validation to Use DNS to Validate Domain Ownership.	November 21, 2017
New content	Added new Java code examples to Using the ACM API.	October 12, 2017
New content	Added information about CAA records to (Optional) Configure a CAA Record.	September 21, 2017
New content	Added information about .IO domains to Troubleshooting.	July 07, 2017
New content	Added information about reimporting a certificate to Reimport a Certificate.	July 07, 2017
New content	Added information about certificate pinning to Best Practices and to Troubleshooting.	July 07, 2017
New content	Added AWS CloudFormation to Services Integrated with AWS Certificate Manager.	May 27, 2017
Update	Added more information to Limits.	May 27, 2017
New content	Added documentation about Authentication and Access Control.	April 28, 2017
Update	Added a graphic to show where validation email is sent. See Use Email to Validate Domain Ownership.	April 21, 2017
Update	Added information about setting up email for your domain. See (Optional) Configure Email for Your Domain.	April 6, 2017
Update	Added information about checking certificate renewal status in the console. See Check a Certificate's Renewal Status.	March 28, 2017
Update	Updated the documentation for using Elastic Load Balancing.	March 21, 2017

Change	Description	Release Date
New content	Added support for AWS Elastic Beanstalk and Amazon API Gateway. See Services Integrated with AWS Certificate Manager.	March 21, 2017
Update	Updated the documentation about Managed Renewal.	February 20, 2017
New content	Added documentation about Importing Certificates.	October 13, 2016
New content	Added AWS CloudTrail support for ACM actions. See Logging AWS Certificate Manager API Calls with AWS CloudTrail.	March 25, 2016
New guide	This release introduces AWS Certificate Manager.	January 21, 2016